JACK'S STORY

A 7th Armored Division Tank Commander in World War II

JOHN H. WILSON

Copyright © 2024 John and Janice Wilson
All rights reserved

TABLE OF CONTENTS

Preface 1
Chapter One: Let's Meet Jack Wilson 5
Chapter Two: Waiting for European Deployment 17
Chapter Three: Transfer to England 25
Chapter Four: France – 9th Replacement Group 33
Chapter Five: Joining the 7th Armored Division 41
Chapter Six: Jack's First Combat Experience 55
Chapter Seven: What's Next? 65
Chapter Eight: German Attack 71
Chapter Nine: The Battle of the Bulge 77
Chapter Ten: Defending St. Vith 87
Chapter Eleven: The Führer Escort Brigade Takes St. Vith . 93
Chapter Twelve: "Fight Your Way Out" 99
Chapter Thirteen: The Retaking of St Vith 105
Chapter Fourteen: Recovery and Return to Service 119
Chapter Fifteen: Crossing the Rhine River 129
Chapter Sixteen: The Heart of the Reich 139
Chapter Seventeen: 7th Armored at the Rim of the Ruhr 145
Chapter Eighteen: The 7th Moves through Germany 155
Chapter Nineteen: Closing the Pocket 167
Chapter Twenty: To the Baltic 175
Chapter Twenty-One: Can't Wait to Go Home 189
Jack's Ending Note 205

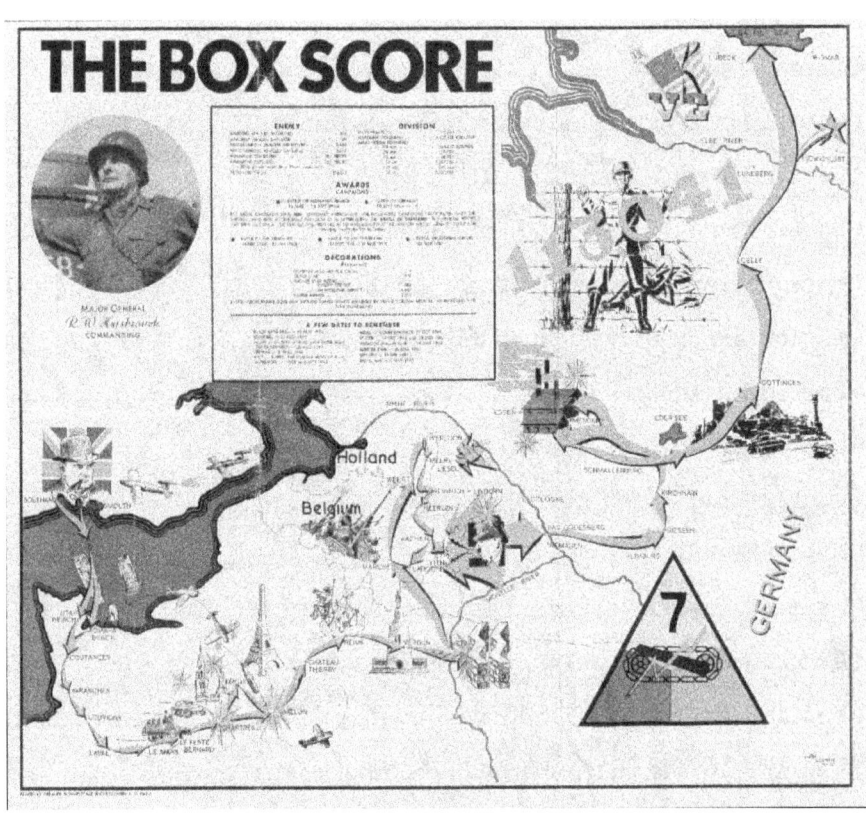

Geographicicus Rare Antique Maps Scan of 1945 Map

Preface

Despite orders to "fight their way out," the Company commander, Stan Nizinski, believed that saving the men's lives and surrendering to the Germans was his only option. He told the Company, "We are surrendering."
Lieutenant Jack Wilson, 1st Platoon leader, disagreed. He pulled his M1911 .45 auto pistol on the commander.

A new generation of kids with parents who had fought in the Great War, believing it was the "war to end all wars," came of age during the Great Depression of the 1930s. Even though they were primarily poor, it was a wonderful time to grow up. They were hopeful and made plans for the future because of their strength of character, belief in God, and the need to work hard to help their families and communities survive their hardships. They looked forward to an education, a great job, meeting the love of their life, and raising a family. They felt blessed to be given all these opportunities.

Their country was attacked when they were only 16 to 25 years old, and they were called to serve and protect the way of life only a patriotic American could understand. They encapsulated what General McArthur later said in his 1962 Farewell Address at West Point: "Duty, Honor, Country."

I am the proud son of one of those kids.

On June 6th, 1944, Allied forces launched the largest amphibious assault in human history, setting in motion the collapse of Nazi Germany and victory over fascism in Europe. Just three months later, my father, Jack Wilson of Seattle, Washington, just 23 years old, found himself deployed to the Western front, joining the 7th Armored Division in the forests of southeast Holland, surrounded by German divisions lurking in the shadows protecting the Westwall of Germany called by the Allies the Siegfried Line. Winter was fast approaching. Like many others, Jack's experience came to be defined by the harsh battles, devastation, and emotions after combat for those brothers-in-arms killed and wounded. These warriors seldom shared stories of these events, particularly with those closest to them. Perhaps they wanted to protect the people they loved most from the harsh realities of the largest and most deadly war the world had ever known. Perhaps it was just too painful to relive. Many memories fade with time, but the trauma of war can haunt a soldier forever.

On the 50th anniversary of D-Day, I wrote my father a letter, which he shared with some friends in the following note.

> To whom it may concern:
>
> I received the following letter from my son John in 1994. I was 73 years old and living in California at my son Willie's home along with Jeannie, my bride of 50 years.
>
> June 3, 1994
>
> *Dear Dad:*
>
> *I have been thinking a lot about you over this last week with Memorial Day and the 50th anniversary of D-Day. I am sure we all have private thoughts about what your generation went through 50 years ago.*
>
> *I have always found it interesting that you have never talked much about your experiences during the war. Seeing a lot of the people interviewed on television about their experiences, they, too, have not shared their thoughts much. I guess it is very true that if you have not shared the horrors of the war that all of you went through, it is difficult.*
>
> *Listening to the various stories about the invasion and the war, I get very choked up. I was fortunate to have not had the experience of war, and I certainly hope that my children do not.*

I want to tell you that this is a special time to remember and to think about what my 23-year-old father was going through, starting 90 days after Normandy.

I love you, and you will always be a hero to me.
John

I had not shared the details of my service with my children, and his letter overwhelmed me as my thoughts returned to fighting in Europe from September 1944 through May 1945.

I shared John's letter with several of my lifelong friends and received excellent responses. My closest friend since childhood, Frank Taylor, wrote, "Jack, you must share your story."

John C. [Jack] Wilson, Jr.

After this exchange, my father did decide to finally reveal his wartime experiences. I hope this story touches the hearts of all who read it and that it reminds us of how young and innocent they all were, and the love and sacrifices made by the "greatest generation" for our country and our future.

John Wilson,
Jack's son

CHAPTER ONE

Let's Meet Jack Wilson

John C. (Jack) Wilson was born in Spokane, Washington. His father's family had migrated to Spokane from Toronto, Canada. They were pioneers in the Washington Territory, supplying meat for the railroad crews building the Great Northern Railroad. In 1916, Jack's father joined General Pershing in fighting against Pancho Villa along the Mexican border and then fought in World War I, returning home as a First Sergeant. His mother's family was from Scotland and Ireland. Her father was a druggist who settled in Spokane in 1908.

When he was 11, in 1932, Jack's parents and his little sister, Carol Jean, moved to Seattle, a young city founded only 80 years earlier by the Arthur Denny Party that traversed the Oregon Trail after leaving Indiana. The Wilsons purchased a modest home on Queen Anne Hill just above Lake Union. They enjoyed views of the growing city, the docks along Elliot Bay of Puget Sound, and of majestic Mount Rainier to the south.

The Depression was devastating to the city's 350,000 residents. Unemployment soared, and many businesses went under, causing the heartbeat of Seattle to come to a dead stop. Thousands became homeless, so that "soup kitchens" became their main source of food, though hardly edible and lacking in life-supporting nutrition.

Hundreds of men lived in a shantytown known as a "Hooverville," named after the former president. It was an unused shipyard south of Pioneer Square. They were very proud men, employed before the Depression, who had lost their homes and, in many cases, their families. They abhorred charity, built shanties, or lived in broken-down old cars. They had their own government, selecting a mayor and agreeing to strict rules, which they enforced among themselves. When the city government or other establishments tried to interfere, they loved to tweak them.

Between the homelessness and so many others having a problem making ends meet, many illnesses plagued the city. One of the most impactful ones was Typhus, which hit many families. At that time, doctors had no experience with the virus, and no medicines were available; they did not know how to treat it. In the Wilson household one of the most devastating things a family could experience happened: Jack's little sister, Carol Jean, was struck with it; she did not survive and passed away when Jack was only 13.

His father was like the other hard workers who prided themselves on doing whatever was necessary for their families and community; one Eastern magazine referred to them as "lumpy and dusty" people. He was a manufacturer's rep for different food products. In 1944, with a partner, he started the Bergoust-Wilson Company, a food canning firm.

In 1935, Jack was entering his first year of high school when the federal government established a new program that would help him afford college. The National Youth Administration (NYA) was a relief agency for unemployed young adults and students. Around the state of Washington, students were paid to work in campus libraries and cafeterias, conduct research, and maintain buildings. By 1937, one in every ten students at the University of Washington held an NYA job.

The University recognized the increasing likelihood of American involvement in World War II and the national economic recovery that would come with wartime production, so it devoted all its effort to supporting the nation as it readied for war.

Jack was accepted to the University of Washington and enrolled in the fall of 1939. The beautiful campus covered over 500 acres in the University District of Seattle. It rose on several hills that looked out over Portage Bay directly south and Lake Union to the southwest.

Jack's goal was to earn a Bachelors degree in Business Administration. He enjoyed his college experience and became active in various organizations. He pledged and joined the Alpha Delta Phi fraternity, working in the kitchen to earn part of his housing expenses. That fall, influenced by his father's military service and a desire to gain leadership skills, he joined the Army ROTC Basic program.

Jack jumped into the many service activities available in his first two years as well as his schedule of classes. His dedication led to his selection at the beginning of his junior year for the Fir Tree Membership Medal, which was given to honor achievement in student activities.

He occasionally joined his parents at the Unity Church at the foot of Queen Anne Hill for the 9:00 a.m. service. After church, he would go to the house for a late breakfast.

On Sunday, December 7, 1941, the church was warm with all the Christmas decorations, and church members were festive; he felt blessed to spend the day with them.

As his mother, Essie, prepared breakfast, his father turned the radio on to the local CBS affiliate, KIRO. It was a little past 10:00, and they were listening to "Spirit of '41," where host John Daley was interviewing guests from the Brooklyn Navy Yard. The two were paying little attention to the radio as Jack told his Dad about what was happening at college. At 10:30, the news program "The World Today" was to begin.

All of a sudden there was a hissing sound for about 15 seconds that drew their attention to the radio. John Daley came back on: President Franklin D. Roosevelt had just announced, "The Japanese have attacked Pearl Harbor by air..."

Carrier-borne planes from Japan had attacked the United States Naval Base at Pearl Harbor, killing more than 2,400 Americans. Eight battleships were sunk or badly damaged, including the USS *Arizona*, which was completely destroyed, and the USS *Oklahoma*, which capsized. Twelve other ships sank or were beached in the attack. Over 180 aircraft were destroyed and 160 others damaged.

The following day, President Roosevelt addressed a joint session of Congress. "Yesterday, December 7, 1941 – a date which will live in infamy

– the United States of America was suddenly and deliberately attacked by the naval and air forces of the Empire of Japan."

The declaration of war on Japan changed everything. Germany and Italy declared war on the United States four days later. There was fear in Seattle of being attacked since it was one of the closest cities to Japan, and blackouts became mandatory.

In March of 1942, President Roosevelt issued Executive Order 9066, and 10,000 citizens of Japanese descent became "enemy aliens" overnight. The federal government removed them from their homes and placed them in detainment camps. Seattle had many Japanese-American citizens who had lived there for almost 50 years.

Seattle's Japanese community was large, with many small business owners running hotels, restaurants, grocers, barbershops, and more. A large group of professionals also included doctors, lawyers, and architects. All the Japanese residents were removed and put into camps. Seattle citizens were outraged because they were an integral part of the city.

Things moved quickly once war had been declared. The draft age dropped to 18, and many men and women immediately left college to volunteer for the Coast Guard, Navy, or Army. Countless men unemployed by the Depression also enlisted or found work in the newly busy armaments factories.

Jack made the decision, as did many of his young friends at the University, to further his training and education in hopes of becoming an officer. In the next 18 months, he would continue ROTC and be commissioned and prepared to serve his country. Some of his fellow students who made the same decision would become lifelong friends through training and their war experiences. They included fraternity brothers Bill Bacon, Dixon Livingston, Jim Castle, and Frank Taylor.

He doubled down on his ROTC training program, studying strategy and tactics. He desired to qualify for the Armor School at Fort Knox, so he devoured everything he could about tank combat.

Jack's participation in the Army ROTC program led to his winning the "Command and Leadership Award" in 1943. This award was given for excellence in leadership, academic achievements, and community service. Governor Arthur Langlie of Washington presented him with a saber to honor his accomplishment.

Jack had volunteered to be a manager of the crew team when enrolling at the university because his favorite sport was competitive rowing. Crew was a big-name sport for the Washington Huskies. In fact, the university's eight-man crew team qualified to represent the United States in the 1936 Berlin Olympic Games, where the team won the gold medal. This Olympic race is still one of history's most famous crew races. It was chronicled in Daniel James Brown's beautiful 2013 book "Boys in the Boat: Nine Americans and Their Epic Quest for Gold at the 1936 Berlin Olympics."

Over his four years at Washington, Jack worked closely with head coach Al Ulbrickson and the famous rowing shell builder George Pocock. As in all sports, teamwork was essential. Pocock said. "Rowing is perhaps the toughest of sports. Once the race starts, there are no time-outs and no substitutions. It calls upon the limits of human endurance. The coach must, therefore, impart the secrets of the special kind of endurance that comes from mind, heart, and body."

Coach Ulbrickson taught that leveraging individual strengths and perspectives would achieve collective success. He referred to it with the phrase, "Individuality is the ace up the sleeve of teamwork."

Jack's crew participation put him in the "Varsity Boat Club" and the "Big W Club," the University of Washington letterman's club.

He studied economics at the start of his junior year and noticed a very beautiful girl who was a sophomore in the class; she really caught his eye. After seeing and talking to her in class, he asked her out. They dated over the next 18 months, and Jean became the love of Jack's life. They were an interesting pair, literally "from opposite sides of the tracks." Jack was from a middle-class family in Seattle, while Jean was from a wealthy family in Spokane. However, they just clicked; Jean was sophisticated with a very dry and fun sense of humor, while Jack was the life of the party.

Francis Jean Fairweather, "Stormy," as her friends called her because of her last name, was born in Spokane, Washington, on April 1, 1922 (six months after Jack), to Han and Nell Fairweather.

Jean's grandfather, Hanford Wentworth Fairweather, Sr., or "Han," was a pioneer in the Washington Territory from New Brunswick, Canada, first arriving in 1871 when he was 28. He was involved with the Great Northern Railroad, real estate, politics, and banking. He was a local Washington Territorial representative to the Territory Convention that approved statehood on November 11, 1889.

Jean's family was fortunate as the Depression had little impact on them. She was an only child and lived an enviable life. The family also enjoyed a lake home at Twin Lakes, Idaho, about 40 miles east of Spokane. Jean spent the summers with her beautiful classic Chris-Craft speedboat.

In her later years Kieran was Jean's only granddaughter, and they developed a close, warm relationship when Jean lived in New York with her daughter, Carol, and her husband, Parker. Kieran had Jean laughing when she asked what Jack was like in college. Did he only go out with you? Grandma said, "He was quite the 'ladies' man,' but he was mine!"

Jean knew that Jack would go into the Army right after graduation, so that their immediate future would be difficult, especially with him going to war. Sure enough, upon graduation, Jack traveled to Fort Knox in Louisville, Kentucky, to start his 17-week Armor Officers Candidate School in basic armor.

He proposed to Jean that summer sending her a caricature (apart but together). They began planning their January 12, 1944, wedding at St. John's Episcopal Cathedral in Spokane. In December, after 17 weeks of training, Jack was commissioned as a Second Lieutenant and would remain at Fort Knox after the wedding.

Jack and Jean were both looking forward to the wedding. On that Tuesday morning, they saw the Dean at the cathedral. After the evening rehearsal, there was a buffet at his aunt Georges's home (his father's sister). The wedding was held on Wednesday evening at St. John's Cathedral; a champagne reception was held at the Davenport Hotel.

The wedding was a formal affair, with the ushers in uniforms or tuxes. Bill Bacon was Jack's best man, and Bayard Young, Bob Ives, Bill Brubaker (Jeanne's cousin), and Jim Castle were ushers. Jean's father had already made train reservations for a Thursday morning return to Louisville. It was a very tight schedule!

Jack cut the six-tiered bride's cake at the reception with the saber he was awarded for "Leadership and Ability to Command."

Cutting the wedding cake with the saber would become a family tradition, with all of Jack's and Jean's children and grandchildren using it to cut their wedding cake.

Back to Work

The couple departed for Fort Knox in Kentucky on Thursday morning, where Jack was attached to an armored training battalion.

Jean shared her impressions of Louisville with Jack's parents – and here one must keep in mind the world she was reared in: "Well, so this is Louisville. Frankly, I'm not impressed. I've never seen such dirt and filth in all my life. Everything is so old here; I can't get over it. I'm so glad I'm with Jack; I don't see how he survived this town alone for five months."

By way of contrast, Jack's update to his parents on Louisville read: "We found a lovely place to live. It is in an apartment hotel. As officers at Fort Knox, we are granted membership privileges at the Pendennis Club of Louisville. Last night, we had dinner and danced to the orchestra that played in the ballroom. At 12, we went to the Louisville Boat Club until 3 AM, then returned to the hotel. We met a lot of lovely kids, and Jean has already been extended several invitations to lunch and dinner."

Jack worked six days a week and spent several nights on base sleeping on a couch.

"He was in bed by 8:00 most nights," Jean reported. She thought "...he was so funny in his sleep; he drives tanks all night, gives orders, and I am black and blue where he has hit me in his sleep. I can't sleep because I am laughing all night long at him. I try to keep out of his way as I figure I can sleep all day, and he can't."

Their grandson, James, read this letter in 2024 and laughed since it explained the habits of his ten-year-old son Collin: "Now I know where his sleeping habits came from!"

Jean got a job as a filing clerk at the Goodyear Rubber Plant. She enjoyed it and was having fun working with the other girls. She was home by noon on Saturday so she and Jack could enjoy his day off. The pay wasn't much, but it was helping with the expenses. She was also delighted with the new apartment.

Between Jack's friends and fellow officers, the new apartment became the fraternity house for Bill Bacon, Jim Castle, Dixon Livingston, and Chris Chrisman from South Carolina, who had become friends with them at Fort Knox. When off base, they would all show up at one time or another. They were all ready to party at the different clubs in town.

Jack's orders arrived on April 4th to report to Camp Cooke on the West Coast on April 18th. Jean left Louisville to return home and visit her parents in Spokane while Jack drove their car to the new base to arrange quarters nearby.

Camp Cooke, 65 miles north of Santa Barbara on the Pacific Ocean, was a 155-square-mile Army garrison established in 1941. The German Blitzkriegs early in World War II had clearly illustrated that a new and more deadly dimension had been added to modern warfare. In response to this new threat, the US Army sought improved training centers to rapidly develop its armored, infantry, and artillery forces. The 11th Armored Division was deployed for this advanced training.

Jack arrived at Camp Cooke on April 17. He thought it was like sitting on a very barren, windy, and cold sandy hill. The weather was so rotten they didn't transition to summer khaki uniforms. "They say that even in summer, it only gets to the low 60s, and the wind is constant at 11 MPH."

He was assigned to Company C of the 22nd Tank Battalion as the maintenance officer. He was called out on his second night with the company because a tank had lost one of its treads. When he arrived with a wrecker and crew, another tank had also lost a track; by the time they repaired the two treads and got them back in, it was 3:30 in the morning. The company had 18 tanks, but only seven were operational; his job was to get them all running!

The training continued with various problems that each platoon had to solve. Several evenings a week they attended officer meetings to discuss wartime strategy and tactics.

Jack wrote his parents about the intensified training they were going through at Camp Cooke. "We are working quite hard here; you can see that this outfit means business. I wrote up a problem to be solved dealing with anti-tank situations, and used dynamite to simulate anti-tank gunfire. The Battalion S-3 Officer (Planning and Training) was quite impressed."

He also gave them an update about Bill Bacon not going with the 9th Armored Division but to Camp Campbell in Tennessee with Jim Castle. Both had been assigned to the 12th Armored Division for advanced tank training.

Jack enjoyed the responsibilities he was given. He became Platoon Leader for the 3rd Platoon of C Company and served on the battalion board responsible for testing the combat ability of the different companies in the battalion. Part of the job was to construct problems for the tank platoons to solve. He found it exciting work and told his parents that he liked it better at Camp Cooke each week.

Jean joined Jack in mid-May after recovering from German measles while at home in Spokane. Due to housing scarcity, Jack and his training friend George Willhoitz decided to share a house to help with their expenses. George and Betty moved in with Jack and Jean.

Jack's Story | **15**

Overseas the war was raging, and Jack knew he would likely be deployed to Europe; it was only a matter of training and time.

At the end of May, they received the exciting news that Jean was pregnant with their first child. Both sets of "grandparents" were extremely excited to hear about their future grandchild.

Several months of training at Camp Cooke went quickly, and Jack received his orders to report to Fort Meade, Maryland, by August 1, 1944. There, replacements for the front were being processed for transfer to Europe and the front lines.

It was mid-July, and they headed to Seattle to spend a few days with Jack's parents, and then to Spokane to see Jean's parents. After Jack headed to Fort Meade, Jean stayed at her parents' home in Spokane, waiting daily for her beloved Jack's letters.

CHAPTER TWO

Waiting for European Deployment

Jack's report date to Fort Meade was August 1st. He flew out of Seattle on the red-eye to Washington, DC, with a stopover in Chicago for refueling, and arrived at 5:30 in the morning. He took the airport bus into downtown Washington and walked for two hours before stopping in a restaurant for breakfast.

Jack thought about Jean and how much he already missed her. Knowing that she was in good hands in Spokane was of great comfort. It was unbelievable to him that he would be a father by the end of the year. "Wow, so much responsibility!"

Around noon, he arrived at Fort Meade, where the War Department had established the American Ground Force (AGF) Replacement Depot Number 1 in 1943. Located between Washington DC and Baltimore, Fort Meade was also a training facility and a POW camp, with several thousand German and Italian prisoners. Over 1.5 million men were shipped from the site overseas, and over 400,000 were processed out of the military there after the war ended.

Jack was assigned to the 5th Battalion, the command for armor replacements headed for Europe.

One can only imagine the logistics of determining what expertise would be needed for troops in battle and getting replacements there at the right time. Being a trained armored tank officer, his deployment would happen in several steps: upon leaving Fort Meade, he would be sent by ship to England and then across the Channel to France, where he would be assigned to a replacement unit for final deployment to a combat unit. He was told it generally took about three months before being transferred to a combat unit between the continued training and transportation.

Garrison military life is pretty standard in any army unit. The little rules are a pain to put up with, as well as acquiring permission for this and permission for that. The 5th Battalion was the same. Jack laughed about needing permission to go across the street to the barbershop. He said that after a while it loosened up, and two nights a week they were allowed to stay out past midnight; the rest of the time, they had to be in by 12:00. Such rules would be short-lived once they were deployed for combat.

Meantime, there was little to do. The wooden barracks were open bays with bunk beds facing the center aisle, just like when he had entering OCS training. Jack had ample time to catch up on reading, something he thoroughly enjoyed, and writing letters to Jean, his parents, other family members, and friends. Jack wrote to Jean almost daily about his experiences at Fort Meade. Occasionally, they could talk on the telephone.

With the country at war, there were few ways for loved ones to communicate. Mail was the primary form of communication in the military, with long-distance telephone and Western Union telegrams being very costly. Air Mail was also expensive, so regular mail was the standard. The military had an efficient mail system, with each unit having an APO (Army Post Office) number.

Imagine, for the moment, the difference in communications today versus back then.

For example, during the war, you could ask, "How is your health? Are you taking care of yourself?" Your wife, if fortunate, would receive that in 10 days. If she responded immediately, you would receive her reply at "Mail Call" in 10 more days at best. Perfection would be a 20-day turnaround. More commonly that conversation would take 30 days! Think about a misunderstanding or misinterpretation of something written in a letter. Talk about having to be careful about what one writes!

In letters home, soldiers were restricted from discussing sensitive military information such as the location and strength of installations, details about transportation facilities, convoy incidents, troop or aircraft movements, operational plans, enemy operations, casualties, or the use of codes. These strictures ensured the safety and security of military operations and personnel.

Letters were given to officers who would review personal correspondence to ensure security. Everyone referred to this as censorship.

Knowing someone would read your correspondence probably made these soldiers' letters the dullest on record. As an officer, Jack found reading others' letters to loved ones the most disagreeable duty assignment he had to endure.

In his letters to Jean, he mentioned that "we do a little or nothing." The day started at 7:00 a.m., and then they stood for roll call at 7:30. Things started getting really exciting with either a clothing check or Bunk Fatigue – slang for reclining on the bed when there is nothing to do.

Many of his OCS classmates were coming into the 5th Battalion, all having gone through the Armor School at Fort Knox together and then assigned to various tank battalions around the country for advanced training and combat readiness.

George Willhoitz, who had shared the house at Camp Cooke, and Cully Culwell from the 11th Tank Battalion, arrived the same week as Jack.

The summer heat and humidity in the Baltimore area were no joke, especially for a guy from Seattle. There, humidity means light rain showers, and summer temps range from the low 60s to the high 70s, a far cry from Baltimore's swelter. In the evening, Jack would find a place outside with a breeze to write his letters and read.

The training continued with trips to the rifle range to fire their M1-Carbines, "Gerard," the regularly issued infantry rifle. On one day, Jack and Cully Culwell went to the range together and bet dinner and drinks. Jack won dinner and five drinks.

What is the old saying in the military? "Hurry up and wait." At last the deployment list was posted, but Jack and George were put on the "alternate" list, where they would most likely have to wait for the next round. Both wanted to ship out as soon as possible. They met with the captain responsible for deployment and asked to be at the top of the alternate list to replace anyone who could not make the current deployment. They were told to check back in a few days.

The war news had been positive since the D-Day landings at Normandy and the fast pace of pushing the Germans out of France. The Russians were also causing the Germans big headaches on the Eastern front. This news caused some of those waiting to go to Europe to have hopes that the war would end sooner than they thought. Jack felt that the sooner they were deployed to Europe, they would avoid deployment elsewhere and could return much sooner to their loving wives and families.

While waiting for final deployment, Jack learned that Cully, George, and he would get a few days of leave. It was time to take a trip to New York City!

When Jack managed Crew at the University of Washington, the Crew participated in the Poughkeepsie Regatta each year against the top rowing schools in the country. Each year, they made the trip to New York City, which Jack loved.

They made reservations at the Edison Hotel in Manhattan. With the heat and humidity August could be tough, but there was no other city like it, and neither George nor Cully had ever been there before. They decided to take the train up to New York on Saturday afternoon, arrived at about 7:00 p.m., and got their room at the hotel.

Jack went downstairs to wire a money order to Jean, and at the Western Union desk met a sergeant named Fred Anderson who had just returned from Italy. They were in uniform, and he told Jack how well he thought of tankers, whom he greatly appreciated. Fred and Jack met up with a Chief Petty Officer, Joe Franklyn, and Major Jim Wilcox, a Marine pilot. They enjoyed a few drinks while swapping stories when Cully and George joined the group for a cocktail. The six of them went to a restaurant that Jim Wilcox recommended. Jack said he had one of the best steak dinners, and a delicious shrimp cocktail with authentic hot sauce. They were all surprised when the bill was only $1.39 per person. "What a fun time we had!"

After dinner, Jack, Cully, and George walked to the Commodore Hotel above Grand Central Station on East 42nd Street and went to the Officers Information Bureau. The Bureau was set up to aid military officers visiting New York City with many services, including giving out tickets to the various nightclubs that were otherwise hard to get into.

They got tickets to three excellent New York City nightclubs: Club 18, El Morocco, and Cog Rouge. Because the three were in uniform, the other club patrons treated them like celebrities.

When they left Cog Rouge on 56th Street, they walked down four blocks on 5th Avenue and went west on 52nd Street to Leon and Eddy's. This was a famous entertainment saloon in its day, and one never knew who would be there. It was loads of fun, and Jack enjoyed it more because George and Cully had never seen nightclubs like these before. They returned to the Hotel Edison, only a few blocks away on 47th Street, just off Times Square.

They slept in until 9:30 Sunday morning, and all felt like hell, so they ordered breakfast from room service. After relaxing, they took a bus to Central Park and walked for a few hours. The heat and humidity were horrible; they were soaking wet the whole time. They could not understand how the people could stand it. They had had to stand in the aisles on the train trip up to New York City, but fortunately, they got seats for the journey back to Baltimore.

That Monday morning, Jack and George went back to visit the captain about going to the top of the alternate list but couldn't get an update. With the rest of the day open, they went to Washington, DC.

They visited the Supreme Court building, the Library of Congress, the Capitol, and the National Art Gallery. At the Capitol, they saw U.S. Senator Wilson of Iowa. George had attended college with the Senator's sons. The Senator believed it wouldn't be long before the war ended. Jack enjoyed the conversation and thought it was fascinating.

After returning from Washington that evening, Jack enjoyed a lengthy telephone conversation with Jean. She and her mother, Nell, were going to fly east to visit New York and Baltimore in hopes of spending time with Jack before he deployed to Europe. They talked about her pregnancy and she shared with Jack that she was exercising, her last doctor visit was very positive, and her health was good.

Nell and Jean arrived in New York, and Jack got a few days of leave and took the train to join them. They had a wonderful time playing tourist in the city. They were able to hire a car service to make it easier for Nell to get around.

They drove to the Wall Street area, where the New York Stock Exchange was located across from George Washington's statue on the Federal Hall steps at Wall and Broad Streets. They had lunch at Fraunces Tavern, where General Washington had said goodbye to his officers at the end of the Revolutionary War.

After lunch, they went down to the Staten Island Ferry pier, which serviced commuters from Staten Island. Next to the pier was the excursion dock for the boats out to the Statue of Liberty. They boarded one of them and had beautiful views back to Lower Manhattan as they passed Governors Island and Ellis Island on their way to the Statue.

Nell was able to book tickets for the Broadway show *Oklahoma*. It had opened the year before and had become one of the most challenging tickets in town. Jack said it was a thrill to experience the Rogers and Hammerstein production at the Saint James Theater on West 44th Street.

Before the show, they had dinner at Sardi's restaurant, which was known for the caricatures of famous people on its walls. The man behind the drawings was Alex Gard, a Russian-American cartoonist. In 1926 he was hired to create caricatures of Broadway and other stars for the celebrity wall at the restaurant. Owner Vincent Sardi and Gard signed a contract stating that Gard would produce caricatures in exchange for one meal per day, an arrangement which lasted until Gard died in 1948. The celebrities included Pearl Bailey, Eddie Cantor, Katharine Hepburn, Leslie Howard, Bert Lahr, and Ethel Merman. A collection of over 200 of Alex Gard's caricatures is now in the New York Public Library for the Performing Arts.

Between sightseeing, dinner, and the *Oklahoma* performance on Broadway, Jean, Nell and Jack had a wonderful day, and called it a night when they returned to the hotel. The following day, they enjoyed brunch and visited the world's tallest building, the Empire State Building. They marveled at its history. It was built in only 13 months during the Depression and rose to 102 stories and a height of 1,454 feet, including its 204-foot broadcast antenna. They took the elevator up to the observation deck, and the views were spectacular.

Jack laughed that being with his wife and mother-in-law in New York City included visiting famous Fifth Avenue stores such as Lord and Taylor, Bergdorf Goodman, Saks Fifth Avenue, and Tiffany's. They enjoyed a wonderful afternoon browsing these beautiful stores. Nell knew Jack was leaving in the morning to return to Baltimore and that he loved steak, so she suggested they have dinner at Gallagher's Steakhouse on West 52nd St.

After their terrific time together in New York, Jack looked forward to Nell and Jean traveling to Baltimore the next week to be closer to Fort Meade and have more time together. Jack wrote his parents about Jean and Nell arriving in Baltimore and getting to the hotel before he did. They spent a terrific day seeing the city and walking two miles, but Jack said that it, "Just about killed Nell! I don't think she has walked that far in years."

"We went to Club Charles and saw a wonderful floor show on Saturday night. Billy Vines was the MC and had just come from the Latin Quarter in New York City. Our table was right next to the stage, and during the show, he looked over and saw Nell. 'Stop the show,' he said. 'Look at this woman over here; she's not much to look at, but take in that four-carat diamond.' From then on, he didn't give her a minute's peace. I've never laughed so hard in my life. Nell was a grand sport and entered right into the spirit of it. When the show ended, he came over and thanked her for being such a grand person. We saw Henny Youngman perform on Sunday night, and he was quite clever."

When Jack returned to Fort Meade after the weekend, he got his shipping orders. He was assigned and immediately dispatched to Armored Company B near Edison, New Jersey, 20 miles west of New York City, for more advanced training before shipping to England. Because of security, he could not see Jean and Nell in Baltimore. He called Jean, told her he was being transferred, and said he would call again in a few days.

CHAPTER THREE

Transfer to England

With the threat of war imminent, in late 1941 the War Department needed a staging ground to ship troops to fight in Europe. A large area of mostly farmland just west of New York City was ideal because of its closeness to the seaports along the lower Hudson River where it emptied into New York Harbor. It was named in honor of the poet Joyce Kilmer, who enlisted in the army and was killed in action in the Aisne-Marne offensive in World War I.

Construction began in January 1942, just weeks after Pearl Harbor, and was completed six months later. They built a small town on 1,500 acres with 1,120 buildings. There were rows of wooden barracks, seven chapels, five theaters, nine post exchanges, a gym, three libraries, four telephone centers, a post office, a 1,000-bed hospital, 28 miles of roadway, and about 11 railheads that fed into the main line. From this staging area, over 1.3 million servicemen were staged and shipped to the European Theater. Jack arrived at Camp Kilmer on Tuesday morning, August 29, 1944, to join Armor Company B.

Jack and Jean talked on the phone while she was staying at the Stanford Hotel in Baltimore. He could not tell her where he was but shared that he was with a great group of men who had a good attitude and were willing to accomplish a great deal quickly.

Jack's Story | **25**

His days were long and busy. He laughed about only having two meals daily, one around 6:30 a.m. and the other at 5:30 p.m. He said he ate Hershey bars the rest of the day, which were getting disgusting.

Jean told him about Nell and their trip to Washington, DC, and how much she enjoyed it. He responded that there were so many lovely historical places to visit there. He was sorry that she didn't have the opportunity to visit the National Art Gallery at the Smithsonian Institute. Of course, he laughed that taking both of those in would take an extra week. It was great to talk, and they looked forward to doing so again in a few days.

He had to spend his evenings censoring soldiers' letters home, reiterating how much he despised having to do that since it felt like such an invasion of privacy. That day, he received a V-Mail* from Bill Bacon (his Best Man), who was already in Europe and sounded pretty low in spirits. Jack wished they could do something to help them over there. The war news sounded good and encouraging. Maybe that would be their prophecy, and the war would end shortly, allowing them all to be able to return. He looked forward to his European assignment and catching up with his dear friend Bill.

*V-Mail: There was a wartime form of US Mail called V-Mail, short for "Victory Mail," which was stationery that could fold and serve as its own envelope. It was a system put in place during the war to drastically reduce the space needed to transport mail overseas.

He got a little time off at the New Jersey post and went to New York City with three lieutenants from his replacement company at Fort Meade: Dan Lunsford, Louis Bresna, and Lester Wilson.

They enjoyed a lovely evening at Sammy's Bowery Follies. It was a famous nightspot with flophouses on either side and panhandlers out in front. The clientele ran the gamut of "down on their luck" local drunks to celebrities from uptown looking to play in the Bowery slums.

Sammy's had an 1890s vaudeville atmosphere, with entertainers putting on a show every night. The joke went that Sammy's was the

"Stork Club" of the Bowery! It was popular with the GIs enjoying New York, and they all got a big kick out of it.

Jack and Jean enjoyed another telephone conversation where he asked that she thank her mother for being so wonderful in looking after Jean for him. Jean told him she felt good and would write often, knowing her letters meant everything to him, as his did to her.

Those telephone calls were important to Jack, along with the belief that the war could soon end and he would be able to return home and get on with their life together.

In another conversation, Jack sensed Jean's voice wavering slightly and asked what was bothering her, and she admitted to being afraid. Jack choked up a little and told her: "My only desire is to finish what I must do and return to you and our family. Sweetheart, keep your chin up. You may be surprised if you answer the door one of these days, not too far off, and you will see me standing there."

It had come time to sail to England.

Company B shipped out of New York Harbor on September 10, 1944, to cross the Atlantic. Jack was pleased he could talk with Jean before boarding the ship; of course, wartime farewells are not for the faint of heart.

In a letter to her, he shared how he felt on the trip over:

The ship was an older British ocean liner and quite pleasant for traveling in September, and the weather was delightful for the crossing, with hardly a cloud in the sky and an extremely calm sea. As you stand by the rail and look out over the vast expanse of water, you recognize how small and insignificant an individual is in the world. There before you is water, crystal blue, nothing else in sight. We saw several porpoises and a whale off in the distance.

The food and service were excellent for the officers, allowing for large meals and putting you in the frame of mind for a good night's sleep. A typical dinner consisted of roast beef, brown potatoes, Brussels sprouts, consommé, and white fish, followed by coffee and peaches on rice pudding for dessert. All you could wish for was available, so no one was hungry. However, the enlisted men did not fare as well as we did.

There is an Officer's Lounge; everybody joins in and sings old-time songs with piano, bass, and guitar accompaniment. Songs like "I Want a Girl (Just Like the Girl That Married Dear Old Dad)," "Wait 'Till the Sun Shines, Nellie," etc. All of us are getting slightly restless and will be glad to arrive at the destination after several nights of it.

Life on board is undoubtedly different for the officers than for enlisted troops. They had rooms below the main cabins and ate in cafeteria-style mess halls. Every other day, the men would come up on deck for calisthenics.

Every evening, the news was broadcast over the wireless. The news about the war effort in Europe was very positive and encouraging; we all prayed it would be over by the time the ship landed.

Jack wrote several letters to Jean during the voyage, telling her that there were things he would remember for some time and would share them when he returned. In most of the letters he tried to comfort her, saying not to be afraid and how much he loved her. Also, with their child's upcoming birth, he told her to be "the little soldier I want you to be."

The others on the ship also wrote to loved ones, so Jack received a stack of mail to censor each afternoon.

The ship arrived in Southhampton on the southern coast of England on September 18th, and Jack was sent to London to await transfer to France.

Britain had been at war with Germany since 1939. After the fall of France, Air Marshal Hermann Goering told Hitler that his Luftwaffe could bomb England into submission so that an invasion was not required. The Battle of Britain was fought furiously for three months, and sporadically for years after, causing devastating damage and the loss of 43,000 civilians, mainly in London, but it did not bring England to its knees. Even in 1944, when Jack arrived, there were food shortages, blackouts, discomfort, and continual V-2 rocket bombings to contend with, none of which caused the British people to be depressed. He found the English resilient, cheerful, kind, and tough as nails!

When our young American soldiers arrived in England, they had heard about the bombings, but this was the first time they had seen the ravages of war. One can only imagine the impact this had on them as the reality of mass destruction was encountered firsthand.

Jack found it interesting to talk with the British people; they were open to conversation and talked about their experiences everywhere they went. At the same time, their graciousness and thankful attitude were humbling to witness. He talked to some about the rocket attacks. It was explained that their warning system worked very well and that the damage was sporadic, unlike what they had experienced in 1940 and 1941. Jack asked about the difference. They responded and told him about a night that London was hit extremely hard:

> The German bombers came a little after dark. The warning sirens pierced the air, alerting us to seek shelter. The sound of the aircraft

buzzed in our ears as the explosions of bombs hitting many London buildings burst into fire; it was all around us. The devastation was everywhere, but we survived; it is not as bad today.

They mentioned how Nazi propaganda told German citizens that they were devastating London, and that the English people believed they were losing the war. The truth in England was, "It is an interruption, and life in London continues unabated."

The ravages of war were evident almost everywhere, but generally everything was well-policed and repaired. "The English people are fascinating," wrote Jack, "although it is difficult to become accustomed to the eccentricities and colloquialisms. They wave at us and will always have a kind word to say." Jack's admiration for the English people was pronounced. In traffic, he noted, the civilians had to sometimes wait for Americans, and they said: "Don't worry, my son, your job is much more important than ours; we shall wait."

How can people like that ever lose!

Then he remembered Prime Minister Winston Churchills' comments to Parliament on June 4, 1940, that said it best in words that still stir every free person's heart:

> The British Empire and the French Republic, linked together in their cause and in their need, will defend to the death their native soil, aiding each other like good comrades to the utmost of their strength. Even though large tracts of Europe and many old and famous States have fallen or may fall into the grip of the Gestapo and all the odious apparatus of Nazi rule, we shall not flag or fail. We shall go on to the end; we shall fight in France, we shall fight on the seas and oceans, we shall fight with growing confidence and growing strength in the air, we shall defend our Island, whatever the cost may be, we shall fight on the beaches, we shall fight on the landing grounds, we shall fight in the fields and in the streets, we shall fight in the hills; we shall never surrender. And even if, which I do not for a moment believe, this

Island or a large part of it were subjugated and starving, our Empire beyond the seas, armed and guarded by the British Fleet, would carry on the struggle until, in God's good time, the New World, with all its power and might, steps forth to the rescue and the liberation of the old.

Having the ability to walk around London was exciting and inspirational. In the Soho district, there was a restaurant called "Victory." It was explained that many restaurants had "victory" in their name, and the menus were Americanized to make the GIs feel more at home. They walked through Victoria Station with the hustle and bustle everywhere. The trains were interesting as they were much smaller than in the United States, and the engines were of a past vintage.

George and Jack were sharing a room in London, and during the evening they listened to "Air-USA," an American station in London. They heard Dinah Shore and Louis Jourdan. It was terrific to hear sounds from home despite the men being gone only a short time.

Even in wartime life continues, and basic needs such as clean clothes do not change. Because of the war, laundry and drycleaning facilities were out of the question in London. The officers washed their pinks (dress pants) and shirts and then had somebody with an iron press them. Jack was running short of clean underwear and shirts, so he did a little washing himself.

They felt London was quite damp, caused by the heavy fog that didn't lift until about two in the afternoon, but they enjoyed getting around and meeting so many wonderful people. They discussed how much they wanted to return to England with their wives after the war.

In a letter to Jean, Jack shared that while walking in the neighborhood he almost picked up a stray dog, but couldn't take him, so he left him behind: "What a friendly little chap."

On Sunday morning, he found a local church and attended the 10:00 a.m. service, which he found very comforting. The congregation members were warm and asked him to join them for tea after the service. It was good to meet and mix with the local London people.

Sunday afternoon, George and Jack shipped out of Southhampton for France.

CHAPTER FOUR

France – 9th Replacement Group

Sunday afternoon, September 24, 1944, onboard the ship, Jack was somewhat bemused that he had not seen his footlocker or bedroll since leaving New York but figured they would eventually show up.

He landed in Normandy on Tuesday morning, September 26th, and spent his first night in a pasture. There he wrote a V-Mail to Jean:

> I thank our Lord that you, those we love, and our country have been spared the ravages and devastation these people, their property, and their country have suffered. You cannot believe its scope until you have seen it yourself.
>
> The local population lives in their barns because the houses have been confiscated by the Nazis and consequently destroyed by Allied forces. Gorgeous cathedrals and churches lie in ruins, destroyed by a defeated retreating enemy. It seems that the Germans, or "Boche" as the natives call them, are particularly obnoxious in this area. One has difficulty understanding what turns educated men into such beasts.

They traveled from Normandy toward the Replacement Group in Fontainebleau, near Paris, on a narrow-gauged railroad. They made many stops where they talked with locals and witnessed the devastation caused by the D-Day landings and the heavy fighting over the previous 100 days.

One of the towns they stopped at was Saint-Lo, a tiny French town 20 miles from the coast held by the Nazis since June 1940. Saint-Lo was a strategic crossroad and served as the center of a crucial German defensive line after the Allies invaded. Taking it would allow the Allies to cut off and control the Cherbourg peninsula to the west as well as open an avenue toward Paris to the east.

The battle for the town was difficult because the area was hilly with lots of vegetation, requiring close quarters combat on the way in. Rather than fences, for centuries French farmers had lined their fields with thick walls of intertwined trees, called hedgerows, each one of which comprised a deadly defensive wall. Saint-Lo was the first of three "battles of the hedgerows," wherein the US Army tried to cut is way forward. The fight for the town lasted for over two weeks and saw some of the bitterest during the war. In the process, US planes had bombed Saint-Lo, targeting the railway station and the power plant. Pamphlets were dropped to warn the residents, but the wind blew them away from the town, causing many civilians to die.

Saint-Lo was 95% devastated and uninhabitable. The battle culminated with Operation Cobra, when the Allies used their strategic bombing force in a rare tactical role to simply obliterate the German defenses. The result was widespread destruction, including hundreds of American troops accidentally caught in the inferno. But the bombers blew a hole through the enemy line. The Germans then bombarded the rest of Saint-Lo as they retreated. It is no wonder why the Germans were hated so much by the French people.

The town got the nickname the "Capital of Ruins." Jack described the place to Jean:

> I was in Saint-Lo, France, or I should say what was once Saint Lo! If you could imagine the combined effects of an earthquake and devastating fire, coupled with the tools of warfare such as bombing,

artillery fire, etc., and then visualize a once fine town left with a few battered walls still erect, debris littering everything, stairways hanging from second and third floors by their carpets, and personal belongings here and there, you would begin to get an idea of what this war is like.

Many more towns suffered in a similar manner, and often, amid such devastation, one will see a house that was not touched. The French we talked to told us of many atrocities the Germans committed in the various communities we stopped in. They feel we are too lenient with them, and after hearing their stories, I'm inclined to believe them.

War is indeed a very vicious and cruel occupation, but apparently, it is the only language that many people understand, hence the need.

At home, Jean was pregnant, and her hormones were raging. Jack was concerned; she in turn was fearful for his safety and what she would do if he had to make the ultimate sacrifice.

Jack recognized this and tried to comfort her as best he could by discussing their faith in God and that he would do all to protect them; however, if something were to happen, he reminded Jean of a conversation they'd had while driving in Spokane the previous July: "Don't forget what I told you. If any accident should occur, my darling, keep the old chin up, lead with a left, and stay in there fighting. Nothing shall happen, but one must always be prepared for any situation."

Jack planned to build a home after the war. He loved the various hills that made up Seattle's landscape, but he was particularly fond of Mercer Island, which sat in the middle of Lake Washington and had views of Seattle. The home would sit above the lake with a lawn running down to the water's edge. He would share his ideas with Jean, hoping she liked them, and then say he could hardly wait to get home.

Interestingly, in 1958, Jack and Jean bought a house on Mercer Island that matched this description to a T.

Most of their letters expressed how they looked forward to their next letter. They also constantly shared how the pregnancy was going and each other's health. If one was in the military, "Mail Call" was truly the high point of the day – if you received mail! He shared the importance of the event: "We were quite fortunate to receive our mail so quickly, and I became the envy of many who have been over longer than me and haven't received any mail yet. It is a huge morale booster."

Jack was stationed for a large portion of October in the French area of Fontainebleau, near the former royal palace, 35 miles southeast of Paris. The grandiose palace had a long history of serving as a residence for French monarchs from Louis VII to Napoleon. The palace also became a German headquarters until liberated on August 24, 1944 by the 5th Infantry Division, part of General George Patton's Third Army. It then became a regional training and replacement pool location. Jack arrived only 38 days later.

The Replacement Pool contained not only new people like Jack, who had just arrived for deployment, but also many troops being reassigned as needs at the front changed. Many had been wounded in action and discharged from the various military hospitals, and were now awaiting redeployment.

Jack was amazed to see how well dressed the French people were. "Most of them were as well off as Americans. We thought they would be in rags. Most people wear wooden shoes because they lack leather and rubber. Their shops are well-stocked, and the only thing the Americans are not supposed to buy, per recent orders, are meals in French restaurants because of the food shortage."

Some of his fellow officers disregarded the order and took to getting steaks, onions, French fries, etc., in the town. "They charge the GIs plenty for anything and tell you when you buy it, 'for you soldiers 300 francs (7 dollars), otherwise 350 francs'." Many people spoke pretty good English: "So you speak English when we go anywhere, then use our best French if necessary. It is quite amusing when you go in and order 'Deus vin rouge' (two red wines). 'Yes, thank you. Anything else?' They have a wine list printed in English. So you can see they were waiting for us, yet our boys have only been here for a few weeks."

One of Jack's great pleasures was playing the piano, and finding the opportunity in Fontainebleau was a lot of fun! He told Jean that he and George, "Went into town and had a few drinks at a joint called the American Bar. I played the piano for a while, and a French violinist went stark, raving mad, and starting to foam at the mouth after violently attempting to match notes.

"We had a gay time, and we immediately dispatched ourselves to the local Red Cross doughnut dugout. They just opened up and have it in a large French home, almost a château. The officers have a nice room in the basement. We had coffee and donuts, bringing two dozen back home, about $.24/dozen. The vultures had devoured one dozen already, and we've cached the others for tomorrow."

There was a gruesome daily occurrence that he had not personally witnessed and hoped he never would. With the help of the French Resistance, the Allied troops had swept across France, liberating towns and villages and unleashing a flood of collective euphoria, relief, and hope. However, this unleashed another horrifying activity: "Epuration Sauvage," a wild purge. It was spontaneous, savage, and unofficial.

The victims were among the most vulnerable members of the community: Women accused of "horizontal collaboration" – sleeping with the enemy – were targeted by vigilantes and publicly humiliated. Their heads were shaved, and they were stripped half-naked, smeared with tar, paraded through towns, and taunted, stoned, kicked, beaten, spat upon, and sometimes even killed. Other types of collaborators were dealt with just as harshly.

Some of the officers in the Replacement Pool were becoming fed up with the delay in getting assigned to a unit, but most were quite content. "It is the easiest life," Jack said, "he had since joining the army." He imagined it would probably be balanced up once he deployed to the front. He strongly felt that no matter what job he was assigned, he would do it to the best of his ability.

George and Jack went into a small nearby town and visited a magnificent Catholic Church. "I cannot describe its beauty except that it is all one could ever imagine and so very old. All the buildings were made of stone or similar construction with slate roofs. Seldom, if ever, do you see a wooden house. It was all so old when compared to United States communities."

Jack observed, "Our men here in France look at the United States in a slightly different respect. The new troops, especially, can see that all at home in the US have no idea what our men are doing here in Europe and what these local people are going through. I have talked to many fellows who have been here since D-Day and D-plus one, some wounded, and others just moving through the Replacement Group. The greatest desire that each shared from their hearts was to beat and utterly defeat the German enemy so that all could return home and never again return to battle."

Jack went to Paris for a day. He wrote Jean, "I'm afraid I am not as cosmopolitan as I try to make out. I enjoyed seeing the Eiffel Tower, the L'opera, La Rue de Paix – shopping, and much more – but was quite frankly disgusted with the rest. The women sought out the American men in Paris, and it was pretty disgusting. All the officers I have talked to have said the same."

Some training was taking place. Jack was giving a class on a captured enemy cannon and had a sergeant demonstrating the piece when suddenly the breach block slammed shut and the sergeant lost a finger. He felt terrible about it, but nobody was to blame, since Jack had his back to him when it happened. He wrote a report about it that afternoon. He said once again, *c'est la guerre* (that's war).

Everybody was delighted to hear about General MacArthur's return landing in the Philippines on October 22nd. This probably meant that no one would have to go to the Pacific when the war ended in Europe.

Jack's friend George received his orders to the front. The two had become close over the past seven months and looked forward to crossing paths again soon. Jack figured he was not far behind and would be joining a unit himself.

Jack was very concerned about Jean's last letter and how she was coping with the pregnancy and their separation. She had attended a party and mentioned how much she didn't enjoy it because of her pregnancy and inability to drink. He tried to comfort her by writing:

> My dearest, you should be so proud that you were bearing a child for us. I wish I could be there to help you adore "him." Please get the idea out of your mind that you are "ugly and fat." It has been time through the ages that a pregnant woman is beautiful; that being a truth, my dear, you are the most beautiful of all. Just think of all the girls and women you have known who would give anything they possess to have their child. I am so proud of you for all you were doing, and the fellows envy me, being a prospective "papa."
>
> Jeannie, remember how Bill Moynahan can enjoy an evening with the folks without taking a drink? Drinking is never essential to enjoying yourself. You must put yourself forward and seek their friendship when you are among people you don't know. That is one of the many doors to success and popularity. With your charming personality and all I love about you, others cannot help but recognize those qualities if you give them half the opportunity.
>
> Remember this always, my darling: when you feel like breaking down and crying, give us one of those old smiles, put your chin up, and show us all.

There had been several dances for the officers, but more needed to be done for the enlisted troops, so Jack and another officer decided to arrange a dance for them too. They used the building that was used as the chapel on Sunday. They arranged it cabaret-style, with a half-moon-shaped dance floor, chairs, and tables for about 350 people.

The Free French group in town sent out invitations for girls to attend. They had help in arranging the wine, and a French woman who owned a café came with glasses, cups, and waiters for the service. They sold beer, and the Red Cross Donut Dugout supplied coffee, donuts, and sandwiches for refreshments.

It was a tremendous success, which Jack shared with Jean:

A GI 14-piece orchestra was really on the beam. All but a few of the men in the company attended the dance; the few that didn't, unfortunately, had guard duty. Over 100 French girls, although some of them were quite young, attended and danced the night away and laughed when they dunked for apples. Everybody had a wonderful time and wanted to know when the next one would be. We gave the orchestra an extra $80 in leftover funds for their work. They have been organized briefly, so giving them the money was nice.

Jack spent much time thinking about Jean and how the pregnancy was going. He had mentioned on several occasions his desire for between four and six children, and Jean was a little surprised by the high number as she had grown up as an only child.

Jack's desire to have a large family stemmed from his childhood memories of his younger sister, Carol Jean, who was called Jeanie by the family. Jack was very protective of her and walked Jeanie to their elementary school, John Hay, which was a 10-minute walk every day. He described her as his best friend and still missed her even after all these years; the memories of their relationship and her death from typhoid would forever be in his heart.

This was during the Depression, and his mother had an understandably difficult time dealing with the death, which impacted their home life substantially.

At last, his time waiting in France was over. Jack received orders to report to the 7th Armored Division in Holland, where he would be deployed for battle.

CHAPTER FIVE

Joining the 7th Armored Division

It was a cold and bitter day on November 11 in Noorbeck, Holland, in the country's southeast corner near the borders with Belgium and Germany, 20 miles north of Liege and 15 miles west of Aachen. The 7th Armored Division was at rest.

Jack was excited to join the "Lucky Seventh" after hearing about some of its actions while in the Replacement Depot at Fontainebleau. He was looking forward to learning from the soldiers about the division and its functioning parts in the various actions and battles they had been involved in.

He was assigned as a platoon leader in Company A of the 17th Tank Battalion, commanded by Lt. Colonel John Wemple. Jack reported to Lieutenant Nick Carter, Company A's commander from upstate New York. Carter had been with the 7th from the time they landed in Normandy. He believed that his new officers should know the division's experiences, both good and bad, to improve his new platoon leaders' knowledge and understanding of how the 7th functioned and fought.

What had the 7th been doing since D-Day?

Lt. Carter started at the beginning. "We landed at Normandy on August 10th. The number of missions we fought in the last 90 days was incredible. Understanding our organization and the battles we participated in is essential. This will give you insight into what you will be doing once you are in combat."

Jack had a fairly good understanding of the division's structure. It had three tank battalions, three armored infantry battalions, and three field artillery battalions, as well as engineer, reconnaissance, signals, ordnance, medical, and headquarters units. He wondered if there was anything unusual he should be aware of.

Lt. Carter continued: "We are organized like all the armor divisions with three Combat Commands: 'A,' 'B,' and 'R' (for reserve). The various combat units rotate between the three commands as needed. Each Combat Command usually operates with three Task Forces. Right now our Company is in CCA, under Task Force Wemple, with our battalion commander as the head of the task force. Being able to change these structures on the fly gives us great flexibility."

Jack was interested in the intensity of the actions in France and asked Carter to tell him what combat had been like after the landing, Over the next couple of days, Carter related the combat stories of the 7th. After coming ashore in Normandy, much of the division was immediately sent east, 190 miles to Chartres, 60 miles southwest of Paris, to spearhead XX Corps of George Patton's Third Army. "We went directly into battle. Our primary mission was to clear the enemy and build bridge crossings at rivers for the Third Army as it pushed the enemy back toward Germany.

"We cleared Chartres, where the Nazis had over 3,000 troops, after 48 hours using two Combat Commands attacking from the east and the west. It was hard fought with a lot of artillery support, and we brutally crushed the defenders, killing many and taking a lot of POWs and equipment. We were able to save their beautiful cathedral.

"We went north to Dreux. According to home newspapers and radio stations, the 'Germans were on the run,' which was the 'biggest victory of all time!' The truth was that our men and equipment were up against a brutal enemy. German headquarters had commanded them to hold the city at all costs. The Nazis finally withdrew.

"We were then ordered to build crossings at the Seine River. CCA and CCB were sent to Melun, a Seine River crossing town 40 miles south of Paris, and CCR traveled 35 miles north of Melun to Point Thiers to establish a crossing.

"The division's 48th Armored Infantry Battalion crossed the Seine River near Tilly, two miles above Point Thiers. The 7th Armored thus earned the distinction of being the first Allied troops to cross the Seine River. The 48th's assault boats and troops were subjected to constant 88mm artillery fire and mortar missiles falling like rain as they crossed.

"Our Allied supporting fire helped the division suffer few casualties by keeping the Germans in their foxholes. After securing the bridgehead, the 33rd Armored Engineer Battalion and the Treadway Bridge Company worked together to construct a bridge across the Seine.

"After getting across the bridge, heavy combat raged from the bridgehead into Melun, and we cleared the town the following day. German defenders were either killed or put into POW cages. 'Paris Radio,' the Nazis' most powerful radio station in Europe, was based in Melun. We took it off the air, and no further broadcasts would exist!

"We then drove 60 miles northeast toward the Marne River and attacked Château-Thierry to build bridgeheads east of the city over the Marne. The Germans fought valiantly to preserve their position and were anxious to hold off our advance. Many Germans were killed and wounded, and prisoners were taken with their equipment due to the bitter fighting."

Jack commented that during World War I, his father had been with the American Expeditionary Forces under General Pershing and fought at Château-Thierry and Belleau Wood.

Lt. Carter continued: "The 7th moved fast to catch up to the retreating Germans, repeating the World War I success! One of our major problems was getting so far ahead of our gasoline and ammunition supplies.

"We traveled northeast to the Aisne River, just north of Reims, the Champagne capital. On 29 August, we reached the river's banks and established a bridgehead that night, taking Reims from the Germans. Verdun was 70 miles east of Reims. On August 31st, soldiers arrived at Verdun's central Meuse bridge shortly after noon and crossed it. The French underground had disarmed mines planted by the Germans. The terrified German garrison couldn't blow up the bridge so they retreated farther east. We took Verdun, the historic city of World War I, without inflicting losses on the local population and with minimal damage.

"During this three-week sweep, we covered 600 miles, the record for a single day being 65 miles. During those 21 days, August 10 to August 31, the 7th Armored Division freed around 150 French towns with over 350,000 people. The Germans thought the rivers would slow the Allied advance. They didn't. We learned a lot and made mistakes, but we were very successful.

"Some would say that the fortress city of Metz stopped Patton's advance, but we thought it was our High Command. All the fuel and ammunition was being sent north for the British effort. The 7th Armored was pulled out of the battle on the Moselle and instructed to move north to Holland to support Montgomery's efforts there, which we can discuss later."

Jack thanked him for the information, appreciated the time, and looked forward to learning more. All that information gave him a perspective, allowing him to think about what his platoon could do.

As Platoon Leader

Jack's platoon consisted of five M4 Sherman medium tanks under his command. One tank was his command vehicle, and two sections within the platoon had two tanks each.

As 1st Platoon Leader, Jack gave orders to the other tank commanders in his platoon while he led with his own tank. He sat in the back of the turret directly behind the gunner, Louie Brodman. In combat, he would call out directions to the driver, Charles Dudley, and targets for the gunner. As the Platoon Leader, he would call out directions to the other tanks, try to sort out what everyone was doing, and keep things under control.

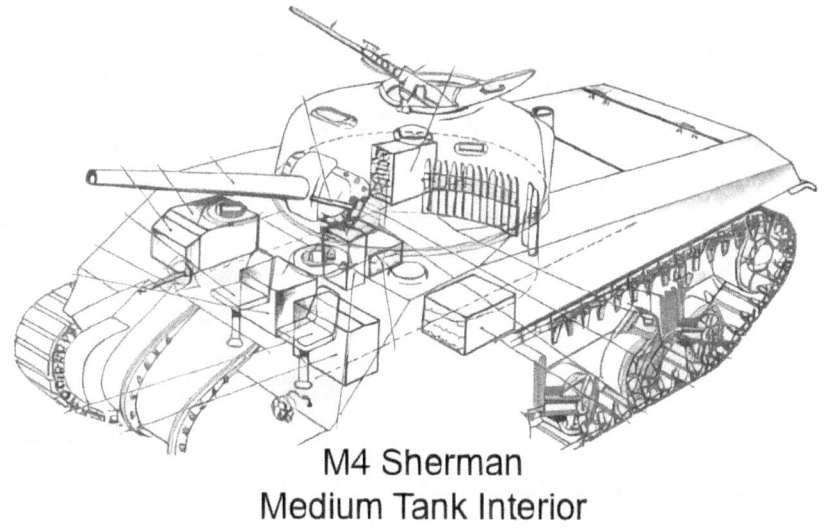

M4 Sherman
Medium Tank Interior

Louie Brodman, the gunner, was positioned right in front of Lt. Wilson, using the same hatch. His primary role was to control the elevation of the 75mm canon, using a combination of a periscope and a direct-view scope. Once the tank commander had nearly lined up a target, it took Louie around five seconds to zero in on it. He also had foot pedals that triggered both the cannon and a .30 caliber machine gun. In comparison, the German Tiger and Panther tanks took longer for the gunner to zero in on a target. The gunner's speed and accuracy were crucial in tank combat, as they could fire off several shots in a short time.

PFC Grant Headburg was the loader who serviced the cannon and machine gun for the gunner. The commander called out the type of ammo to load. Once loaded, the loader yelled, "Up!" Letting the gunner know the cannon was loaded. He made sure the machine gun had ammo and was trained to quickly fix any problems with either the main gun or machine guns. His position in the turret was to the gunner's left, where he had a lot of space to work. In combat, he was very busy keeping up with the gunner.

Both the driver, Charles Dudley, and the assistant driver, Mike Anderson, were located in the forward part of the tank's hull. With his limited vision, the driver relied on the commander's directions for navigation. However, he also needed to anticipate obstacles and understand how the tank would react. The assistant driver, positioned on the lower right side in the "bog," had a .30 caliber machine gun and was responsible for maintaining a lookout using his periscope. Despite being the "low man on the totem pole," his role was crucial in ensuring the tank's safety and effectiveness in combat.

Jack had all the roles for his team in place, and he had learned much of the information while he was at Camp Cooke in California, doing his advanced training, and while creating combat problems for the various platoons to solve. He worked closely with Master Sergeant Al Meyerson, who had served under General Patton in Africa. Meyerson took him aside one day and gave him some advice.

"Your combat team has one question about any new young officer: Would he get them killed?

"You will not have seen combat, and the regular combat troops want to be assured that the new officer isn't set on the glory of killing the enemy and making a name for himself. They want to see that you can do your job and not be a 'glory hunter' by nature. You must know that junior officers must earn the respect of their men.

"Work hard to be a good commander and encourage your crew to be as good as possible. Treat them with respect. Know that a tank crew is interdependent, and everybody has to do their job as best they can. When you finally get your platoon command, listen closely and take the advice of your senior NCO. Let him command your platoon until you get some real leadership experience. You will gain the confidence required to command in combat."

Staff Sgt. Glen Piontkowski was Jack's senior NCO (non-commissioned officer) and second in command of the platoon. He had been with Company A since Omaha Beach. Jack sat down with Sgt. Piontkowski and let him "show him the ropes."

Jack thought this advice was an important life lesson and later shared it with his kids and grandchildren. This was the comment from Chris, one of his grandchildren who joined the Coast Guard: "Something I remember Grandpa saying to me when he lived with us in Benicia that resonated with me through my career was, 'Always trust your NCO.'

"During my time as an E6 and E7 in the Coast Guard, I encountered many situations in which the phrase 'always trust your NCO' resonated with me, and my instinct and intuition proved correct when advising senior officers. One thing he told me: later in life, I would appreciate its importance.

Jack wrote a letter to Jean that first night:

> Guess who is in the battalion? Remember Chris Chrisman from South Carolina? It was like an old home week. I also knew about five other officers here, so I had some friends to get me started right.
>
> Many of the men in my company have the Silver Star and other decorations. They are a grand bunch of fellows and have been through a lot of fighting. My commanding officer told me about what they did in France; these guys are amazing. I am so excited to be part of them.
>
> We're out in a muddy field, but today, we moved into some barns, and it is much warmer and dryer than before. Remember us in your prayers.

The 7th Armored was primarily at rest for the next few weeks. This was their first relief from constant combat since arriving in France. Just like Jack, there were many new replacements in the outfit.

Sgt. Piontkowski asked Jack if Lt. Carter had told him about what the Division had gone through, and Jack told him about their conversation. The sergeant suggested that Jack ask him about Holland because, in many ways, it was different from France. He said he would.

The 7th Armored in Holland

While still in England Jack had heard about the spectacular opening of the campaign in Holland, with Field Marshal Bernard Montgomery launching the largest airborne assault in history. But it had ended in disaster, with the British 1st Airborne Division nearly wiped out at Arnhem, and US airborne divisions alongside British armor and infantry bogged down. It was into that maelstrom that the 7th Armored had been transferred from Patton's army to assist the campaign up north. Jack caught up with Lt. Carter later in the day and told him he would like to hear about the different actions in Holland.

The lieutenant had time and told Jack that Holland had been an entirely different experience from France. Here the Germans were no longer in headlong retreat, but closer to their own border were holding on to every village, marsh, dike, and woods. Carter gave a short overview of what was going on with the British, and the strategic problem of the sector.

"Allied supplies primarily came in via the port of Cherbourg in France and the beaches at Normandy, creating long trucking routes to the front. You would be amazed that delivering one gallon of gasoline to the front took five gallons of fuel."

If the Allies could capture the port of Antwerp, it would solve their mounting logistical difficulties because the port could handle 1,000 ships at a time carrying 19,000 tons each. Antwerp had 10 square miles of docks, 20 miles of waterfront, and 600 cranes. While the British had captured the port from the Germans, "...their mistake was not realizing it was 80 miles from the open sea via the River Scheldt, bordered by islands on the north and the south, and that 50,000 German troops had move in to control the seaward islands. The port could not be used."

British, Polish, and Canadian forces were responsible for clearing the Germans from the islands and putting the River Scheldt under Allied control. The 7th Armored Division was to defend its southern, or right, flank. "This was a first for the 7th," continued Lt. Carter, "providing defensive support. There were a few battles with the Germans to gain advantageous positions and local battle victories. Still, most of the time was spent watching the canal-striped flatlands for potential problems.

"While the fight for the Scheldt Estuary was underway, we joined forces with the Brits to move north against the Germans in what would prove to be brutal fighting through October and into November. Our mission was to clear the Peel Swamp west of the Maas [Meuse] River.

"The Peel is a region in southeast Holland, best known for extracting peat for fuel since the Middle Ages. The towns' names were generally the family names of the peat company owners. The area is a swamp with many canals dug over the years for boats to take the peat to market. The Germans used the Peel as a defensive line against the Allies moving north.

"On September 30th, Combat Command B was a striking force that moved north toward Vortum, Holland, about 80 miles northeast of Antwerp. The units encountered strong enemy bazooka and anti-tank fire along the route toward Vortum and overcame it by wiping out the defenders. The leading elements captured Vortum on October 2, and we liberated our first Dutch town.

"Simultaneously, CCA attacked Overloon, another small town in the Peel. Overloon was heavily defended by German paratroopers and former Luftwaffe personnel from well-prepared positions. As the fighting continued, the British 3rd Infantry Division and their 11th Armoured Division joined us for what became known as the Battle of Overloon, which lasted from September 30th until October 18, 1944.

"The assault on Overloon led to heavy losses for both us and the Brits. The 7th Armored was reassigned to the British Second Army, and they continued the assault with tanks. The British and Germans engaged in the largest tank battle on Dutch soil, with heavy losses on both sides. The Allies finally eliminated the German bridgehead west of the Maas.

"The 7th's next assignment was to cover a 22-mile front with the town of Meijel, 70 miles east of Antwerp in the center of a line running north and south along the canals. The line consisted of several outposts with a few men, each sometimes as much as 800 yards apart. Many German patrols had been active in the area. Bad weather had kept Allied air support grounded. German intelligence must have been aware of our precarious position along the 22-mile front because on October 27th, the Germans launched a counterattack to disrupt what the British were doing at Antwerp.

British Second Army Commander Miles Dempsey recognized the strength of the German counterattack, ordered additional forces into the battle, and asked the 7th to hold the line. "We were outnumbered three to one and gave up little ground. The German dead littered the battlefield and were proof of our effectiveness. There had been some withdrawal to protect the troops and equipment; however, the major accomplishment was that the Germans had not gotten through. Still, our General Sylvester was relieved of command, and General Robert Hasbrouck took over command of the 7th Armored.

"They then moved us a little south next to the British VIII Corps to take over a narrow sector south of Meijel, centering on the small canal junction at the town of Nederweert. The Jerrys were dug in everywhere and had strewn mines of every description in preparation for the Allied advance. This made the initial advances very slow. The Germans on the north side of the canal furiously fired from their dug-in artillery and tanks. With British air support and the 7th's artillery, the harassing German forces were soon silenced. The battle was now under control, and on November 6th, the British VIII Corps released us back to the US Ninth Army.

"And here we are, welcoming you to the 7th!" Lt. Carter concluded. Jack thanked him and felt he had a greater understanding of the people he would go into battle with. He knew they would have his back; and he would support them with all he had to give.

Combat Training

Colonel Wemple's battalion training program lasted over ten days. With so many replacements, preparing the units for combat and for working as teams was essential.

The 17th Tank Battalion commander was a firm believer in the "basics." There were instructions and practice in target designation and fire orders to make the crew's first artillery shot accurate. Col. Wemple insisted that all crews be trained to give fire orders as prescribed by the training manuals; all crews were to be drilled on this until the orders were automatic.

Communication in combat with the attached infantry was critical to success, and Jack's platoon and Company A worked on a "Tank-Infantry Communications Problem." They were paired with an infantry company from the 38th Infantry Battalion.

Some of the tankers, including Jack, referred to their infantry partners as "doughboys" out of respect. This was the term mainly identified with the US infantry in the Great War, in which Jack's father had fought. More commonly the infantry in the Second World War were called "GIs," a term that may have derived from the stamp of "Galvanized Iron" that was seen on so much army equipment; others claimed it simply stood for "Government Issue."

The tanks were equipped with telephones on their outer hulls, so the infantry could communicate with the tank commanders. The tank platoon leaders' radio was on the Infantry Company Commanders' channel, so infantry officers could inform the tank commanders by radio of "on the ground" intelligence or where the tanks were needed.

The problem demonstrated how effectively tanks could be called up to overrun machine-gun positions and thus protect the infantry, or how effectively infantry could be used to envelop AT (anti-tank) gun positions and thus protect the tanks. The exercises were essential training, and all troops greatly benefited from it.

As you can imagine, keeping the men as clean as possible with showers and laundry was a quartermaster's challenge. While the training was in full swing, the battalion sent 30 men and officers to the nearby city of Maastricht for showers. Staff was rotated until all had been accommodated. Quartermaster laundry facilities were available so the men could get their clothes cleaned and put in good condition. This continued daily until the whole battalion could clean up.

By November, trench foot had become a major medical issue in the wet, cold, muddy fields. Many in the battalion had developed trench foot, so the medical officer ran classes to avoid the problem. They kept their feet as dry as possible by washing them and changing their socks frequently. When signs of trench foot developed, the individual was sent to the medical detachment. They kept his shoes off his feet for 24 to 36 hours, usually clearing up the problem.

The 7th Armored supported the General William Simpson's Ninth Army, preparing to move into Germany and capture the important Ruhr Valley, an industrial center where a significant portion of Germany's military support equipment and armaments were manufactured.

The Battalion commander received top-secret information regarding these possible future actions that the Battalion would support. Many officers were briefed on available information about the terrain they might be committed to and instructed to carefully map all areas to the front, along with available enemy information, to pass on to the other officers and men.

The Battalion scheduled another joint training session with infantry platoons on November 16th and 17th. The mission was to capture a town utilizing two tank platoons – 10 Sherman tanks, abreast of each other – followed by two armored infantry platoons mounted on half-tracks. Another platoon of infantry and a platoon of tanks would follow as a reserve.

The problem was set up using two Dutch towns for the exercise. It started in Hoogcruts to the south and moved north two miles to Reijmerstok.

The right assault platoons enveloped Reijmerstok to the east and northeast, while the left assault platoons flanked the town to the west and secured approaches from the west and north. The reserve platoon of tanks and infantry entered Reijmerstok and cleared out the enemy. The force commander used his supporting weapons when and how he needed them.

The problems and the plans were simple and designed to emphasize the basic fundamental principles involved in combined tank-infantry operations, and they accomplished just that.

Jack enjoyed participating in the training exercise as it put his Stateside training into more vivid perspective.

During the night, an endless number of robot bombs had been sailing over their training area and falling not far from their encampment. These were German V-1 flying bombs, designated Vergeltungswaffe (vengeance weapon) 1. They sailed overhead and made a peculiar sound; the English called them Buzz Bombs because of their pulsating sounds.

Jack's work schedule kept him outside most of the day, and by 6:30 in the evening, he laughably said: "I can hardly keep my eyes open. The spirit of fellowship and the favors people did for each other was heartwarming."

His friend, Lt. Chris Chrisman, one of the frat boys from Fort Knox, had dropped in for dinner that night and given Jack a combat suit that was very difficult to obtain; he was very grateful.

He told Jean that he appreciated the "Company's First Sgt., Robert Johnson, who went out of his way to get me some airmail-stamped envelopes. The men called the first sergeant 'first soldier' because of the example he set and how he performed his duties. What an inspiration!"

Dealing with the local Dutch people was a pleasure, though sometimes challenging as a local Dutch fellow he met wanted to be part of Jack's tank crew, and it was a little tricky talking him out of it. He told him there was not enough room in the tank for another man. Jack guessed he'd catch on before long. It was interesting how much the locals wanted to be involved in helping the United States.

Jack enjoyed the families he became billeted with and how kind they were. He was staying with a Dutch couple near Noorbeck. When he left the command post and went to the house to sleep each night, the woman had a big pan of hot chocolate waiting for him. It was nice, but he had to get up thrice a night, which wasn't good.

There, it was proper to call the wife of a mayor or army officer "Mecha Frau" and the wife of other people "Madame." Jack called this lady Mecha Frau, and she blushed very coyly!

To his wife Jean, he commented, "To prevent any alarm on your part, darling, she is about 50 or 65. She did my washing and scrubbed my muddy boots, and I couldn't pay her, so I gave her some soap."

The first ten days with the 17th Tank Battalion had given him a chance to know his platoon and the other officers in Company A as well as several of the officers in the battalion. He ended the evening with a letter to Jean:

> My vehicle is brand new and slightly bigger than the ones you've seen. It's a sweetheart, and we are quite satisfied. I hope the Jerry's feel likewise because we "aim to please."
>
> Concerning the child's name, I can only say that Peter does not appeal too much, but if you like it, that is my choice. I might suggest William, Dixon, or Robert. Perhaps I am too much of a conventionalist. Having a "III" on the kid is rough, as I've known a few. Use your best judgment, darling.
>
> More later, old girl, take the best care of yourself. Pray for us!

CHAPTER SIX

Jack's First Combat Experience

Allied Goal: "Cross the Rhine"

The time had finally arrived. With all the training behind him, Jack was about to enter battle for the first time. He felt confident but at the same time feared what might happen.

The 7th Armored Division's actions from August through the beginning of November had involved constant combat in France and Holland. General Omar Bradley (Commanding General of the 12th Army Group) wanted the 7th to be refreshed and rested for its next significant engagement. They spent time replacing troops, including Jack, and re-equipping the division. Every unit of the Lucky 7th continued to train for future combat. Thorough preparations for a new offensive against the Germans were being implemented for Jack's first deployment.

In late October, Eisenhower met with Montgomery and Bradley to discuss strategy against Germany. They planned to continue the significant effort to continue east into Germany and cross the Rhine River. This would allow the Allies to envelop the Ruhr industrial region, where 80 percent of the Nazis' aircraft, trains, military equipment, and ammunition were produced.

The initial goal was to clear the German Army back to the Roer River. This meant it was also necessary to capture and control the Roer River dams that could be opened anytime, flooding the lower areas that would trap the Allies if they attempted to move toward the Rhine.

Operation Clipper

A joint British and American effort called Operation Clipper had started on November 18th with the mission of clearing the Geilenkirchen salient, which was part of Germany's western defenses.

The Westwall, called by the Allies the "Siegfried Line," was 400 miles long on Germany's western border, built to stop or slow down any invasion from the west. The fortifications consisted of three-foot-high concrete obstacles called "dragon's teeth," along with many supporting "pillboxes" that were like mini forts for troops to live in. The dragon's teeth were often wired with explosives, surrounded by mines, and covered by Nazi machine guns and artillery power.

Various units of the 7th, such as the 17th Tank Battalion, which included Jack's Company A, were temporarily assigned to the Second British Army to support its efforts to reach the Roer River. The German defenders fought hard, and the landscape contained many small towns providing refuge to the Nazi fighters. The effort was slow as larger towns, such as Geilenkirchen and the ancient city of Aachen, took up to a week or more to clear.

7th Armored Intelligence reported that elements of the German 10th SS Panzer Division were active in the area. They had tanks in Lindern, Germany, three miles northeast of Beeck. This concerned the 84th Infantry Division, also assigned to the British.

Intelligence also reported that there were many tanks in the town of Beeck. The enemy continued to defend the pillboxes in this sector very stubbornly. The enemy defended the Beeck sector with an estimated six infantry battalions or paratroops acting as infantry, supported by at least two companies with anti-tank guns.

With this intelligence, the High Command decided it was best to clean out the town of Beeck as it was the most southern and closest to where the 84th Infantry Division was located.

Company A to Attack Beeck

Colonel Wemple, commander of the 17th Tank Battalion, ordered Company A to support the 84th because Lt. Carter, Jack's commanding officer, had reconnoitered this area to defend against a German counterattack, if necessary, and was familiar with it.

The 84th Infantry Division ordered Company A to coordinate an attack on Beeck with the 405th Infantry Regiment's 2nd Battalion.

Lt. Carter met with the commander of the 2nd Battalion, who thought that the enemy in Beeck could be easily overcome. He believed no more than four enemy tanks were in the town that day.

Lt. Carter told the commander that he had twelve medium tanks and one 105mm self-propelled (SP) assault gun, which he would use in the attack. Returning to his company's assembly area in Prummern, he addressed his officers and NCOs on the mission: "The 2nd Battalion commander of the 405th Infantry has just briefed me. Let's discuss our attack plans. We will move out of the assembly area, skirt the town to the west, and secure the area.

"We will attack with two platoons abreast, commanded by Lt. Wilson and Lt. Nizinski, with four tanks each and in line. Lt. Williams' platoon with its three tanks will be in reserve. The assault tank and my tank will follow close behind the assault wave. The assault gun will be directly under the Battalion commander's control of the 405th…Any questions?"

Jack understood the orders presented, as the action would be similar to a scenario they had practiced a few days earlier.

The Attack Begins

The Company moved into position among the orchards on the east side of the town of Prummern. They traversed along the orchards, using them for concealment, moving eastward towards Beeck through the dense apple orchards and then out into more open fields to prepare for the attack against the entrenched German armor and infantry.

The weather had been ferocious. It was bitter cold with strong winds. It had rained for the last three days, making the ground very soft. The worst problem was the mud. It was like clay; if you put your foot in it, it clogged around your boot, slowing your ability to move. The mud was not considered in the original plan but had to be dealt with.

As they moved forward, one of Lt. Nizinski's tanks got bogged down. As they continued north, Jack lost two tanks that got stuck in the mud. Both platoons continued. Lt Carter's tank ran into a ditch and turned over.

Lt. Carter immediately exited his tank, climbed into the SP assault gun, and resumed command. Lt. Williams' reserve platoon was in the orchard area and started to move forward to support both Wilson and Nizinski when his tank got stuck. He then lost the two other reserve tanks to the mud.

At 2:30, Lt Carter, who had started with twelve tanks, had only five left, plus the 105mm assault gun ready for the attack. He initiated the attack, as ordered, with the few tanks remaining under his command.

Supporting elements and the 75mm guns on the Sherman tanks used smoke cartridges to conceal their movement from the enemy as they moved forward.

Under the smoke's protection, they moved relatively quickly toward the higher ground. The smoke cleared as they passed beyond the hill, and they engaged the enemy in a fierce firefight. Jack commanded the left platoon, which now included only his and one other tank. Lt. Nizinski commanded the right platoon, which still had three tanks. Lt. Carter proceeded to the left of Jack's tanks with the 105mm SP gun.

They started receiving heavy artillery, anti-tank, and small arms fire from the town of Beeck to their front. Heavy fire was also coming from the high ground to their right.

As the tanks passed through the 405th Infantry, they were not followed as planned. What happened?

It turned out that the 2nd Battalion commander of the 405th had mounted his command tank and moved into position but it was hit by an artillery shell, knocking out his communications equipment. He was to coordinate with his infantry commander on the ground and coordinate the attack as much as possible. He finally contacted his infantry unit on a backup radio, but the attack had already been launched, and there was no infantry coordination with Lt. Carter's tanks.

Lt. Carter's tank continued to engage the enemy until it received a direct 88mm hit on the turret at about 3:00 in the afternoon. The tank exploded and there were no survivors. A few minutes later, Lt Nizinski's tank was also hit by enemy fire and knocked out of service. He and his crew were able to bail out.

Jack's platoon was to the right of Carter and continued to engage targets of opportunity. They fought "not buttoned-down" but with hatches open. A German shell ricocheted off the periscope on Jack's tank, throwing him to the bottom of the turret.

Climbing back into position, he saw a German Tiger tank emerge on his right front, from where they had been taking fire. Wilson directed Louie Brodman, his gunner, to load a white phosphorus shell and aim at the Tiger's turret ring. He waited as loader Grant thrust the shell in the breech, and Cpl. Brodman took aim at the Tiger. Jack's instructions to "fire" were executed, and the shell hit the Tiger's turret with flames and smoke.

There was no chance of penetration, but the shock within the Tiger must have been horrific. The entire area above the driver's compartment was covered with burning white phosphorus. The Tiger's engine fan sucked the smoke into the main compartment. The Tiger's crew must have believed their tank was on fire and abandoned it.

Jack looked around and found he was alone! All the other friendly tanks in Company A had pulled back toward the infantry. He commanded his driver to make a zig-zag reverse retreat and joined the other tanks behind the 405th Infantry Battalion.

By 5:00 p.m., it was getting dark, and higher headquarters ordered that all Company A's tanks that could move must return to the battalion assembly area. The Company would then revert to 17th Tank Battalion control.

The A Company team had entered this battle with three platoons, 12 tanks, an SP gun, and 60 men. They returned with two tanks and the ten men operating them. Five men were killed when Lt. Carter's tank was hit, and 45 men were able to escape their abandoned tanks. Jack experienced not only his first action in battle but the heartbreaking loss, for the first time, of comrades in arms.

When he arrived at the assembly area, the Battalion Service Company served Thanksgiving turkey to the crews in their tanks.

Report on Operation Clipper

The After-Action Report read, in part: "A flanking attack by the 405th Infantry toward Beeck with the support of Company A of the 17th Tank

Battalion on 23 November also became bogged down against prepared Nazi defenses. British assaults on the other side of the Wurm River were also beaten off by strengthened resistance.

"Despite the frustrations of 22 and 23 November and the failure to capture the final objectives, the purpose of the operation had now been achieved at an Allied cost, including 2,000 US casualties, 169 killed, and 752 missing in action.

"The Geilenkirchen salient had thus been effectively removed. The 84th Division reverted to US control, and further attacks were abandoned."

This being Jack's first combat experience. He wrote letters home, but some information about the battle was not shared with his mother or loving wife, not wanting to worry them about his safety. The ability of all these young men to compartmentalize these horrendous war experiences was astounding.

> Dear Jean,
> This is my first chance to drop you a line, so I will catch up with "what's new."
> War is indeed a cruel and ruthless business. I am thankful that you and those we love are spared the sights that are ours each day. I have seen the loss of life, the destruction of homes and equipment, and the destroying power of weapons, and it all adds up to "no good."
> I am writing this from a German pillbox deep in the Siegfried Line. I'll bet that Jerry never thought the day would come when the Yanks would sleep in his forts. At any rate, we are quite comfortable and not in any danger presently.
> We had turkey for Thanksgiving, and although I was not in the mood to eat, I had more to be thankful for on this particular Thanksgiving Day than any since I can remember.
> Yesterday was Sunday, and I went to church in a building that was formerly a Hitler Youth Center. The chapel reminded me of the scenes in "Mrs. Miniver," the bombed church. We sat on our helmets

and listened to a sermon on the miracles of Christ and how he fed the 5,000 from the five barley loaves and two small fishes. The chaplain was an Infantry major and conducted an outstanding service.

On Friday, about 14 of your letters arrived, and I was kept busy while reading them. They mean so much to me.

I just took a walk to give my boys the password for tonight and then censored a few letters, so I will finish this and get some sleep.

My darling, I have relived our time together many times since coming over here, and when I return to you, we shall pick right up where we left off. I miss you very much and love you with all my heart. I must close for now. I will write more tomorrow.

Love,

Jack

Jack did share a few short notes with his father, which expressed his feelings about combat:

4 December 1944

Dear Dad,

Just a note to you on the side. I feel like getting a load off my chest and always burdened you with it, so here it goes:

I don't know how to start, but the idea is like this. Our job here is more rugged than I ever could have imagined. My first engagement netted me one Tiger Tank, but I came out so damn scared and upset I couldn't eat the turkey for Thanksgiving.

So far, I've managed to keep out of the way of Jerry's 88s and intend to keep doing so if possible, but I have a hell of a time stomaching the deal, especially when you see our boys and Jerry's stacked up like cordwood. I can't see any reason in the world why men have to kill each other to prove a point or two.

I haven't lost my nerve, so don't misunderstand me. I just don't like the damn deal and can't get out of it soon enough. We'll sweat it out together, pops, and if something unforeseen happens, I know you will help Mother and Jean along for me. I've got the old boy chin up and think of you as my guiding star.

    Love,

    Johnny

Ten days later, he shared other thoughts with his father on 14 December 1944:

> I had a bull session with my driver, Tech Sergeant fourth class Charles Dudley, a wonderful fellow from Virginia, and I like him very much. He is 34 and claims he is a confirmed bachelor. We have been discussing our California service and how times have changed. I wonder if things will appear the same to us when we return home as when we left. The boys are talking about bailing out of tanks after being knocked out. Nice subject. Eh! Oh well, such is life.
>
> When I think of men's lives that depend on my judgment and actions, I sometimes feel that the job is too big for me. I couldn't take this sometimes if it weren't for all you've taught me and my faith in our Lord. I get so upset I can't eat or sleep, but God takes care of us, and if I have my way, all of my boys are returning to their families and loved ones. I pray to God that this ends soon.

With the end of Operation Clipper, the 17th Tank Battalion was reattached to the Lucky 7th. Some units, like Company A, continued to provide artillery support for various units of the Ninth Army.

Jack read the letters he received from his parents and Jean. She was due with their first baby shortly, and he was so happy they were all doing well at home. It was such a morale boost for him.

He also had many thoughts about what the enemy was up to, as German activity seemed relatively quiet in mid-December.

CHAPTER SEVEN

What's Next?

As many like Jack in Company A wondered, "What is next?" it is essential to examine what the Allies were up to and, of course, the countermoves of Hitler's Wehrmacht.

The Allies had made a significant effort in preparation to move east from the Roer River to reach the Rhine River. They continued to watch the Sixth Panzer Army setting up defensive positions around Cologne, getting ready to defend against the Allied attack on Germany. The intelligence they gathered from neutral and other Allied sources discussed a central German defense of their homeland.

Many Allied troops were in the northern area waiting for the kickoff. Much thought had been given to what Hitler was up to and if he would make any move other than defend the Ruhr Valley.

Some rumbling of intelligence came from the Ardennes Forest that was discounted out of hand. The Allied commanders had discussed the potential of a German attack there but believed it unlikely because of the rough terrain with small roads crisscrossed by many streams and rivers. The weather in November and December comprised another challenge. This mountainous country had much rainfall and deep snow. The raw, harsh winds swept across the plateaus. The mists were frequent and heavy, lasting into the late morning before breaking up. Predicting this weather was difficult at best – average days of freezing weather ranged from 113 days in Malmedy to 145 days in Bastogne.

Besides, all intelligence pointed to a German defense of the Ruhr Valley.

Over the past few months, the Ardennes became known as the Ghost Front. The Siegfried Line ran along portions of it. The Americans and the Germans were relatively short distances apart, and there had been little fighting between them, maybe a morning artillery blast from either side to let the other know "I'm here."

Both sides used much of the Ghost Front, 80 miles in length, as a rest area for combat units rotated out of heavy fighting and a location for new units that needed time to prepare for their first combat actions.

The American forces occupying the Ghost Front included the brand new 106th Infantry Division, which had recently landed in Normandy and was driven by trucks in the cold rain to the Schnee Eifel. Their clothing and equipment were not geared to cold winter conditions. When they arrived the available billets were rain-soaked and needed work before troops could use them. The troops suffered from trench foot, frostbite, and just miserable conditions. They replaced the 2nd Infantry Division, which was being rotated back to combat. Typically, an infantry division would cover a front of five miles. The 106th and the attached 14th Cavalry Group covered more than 21 miles of front. It was very weak.

To the north (left) was the 99th Infantry Division, another new unit from the United States, part of V Corps, as well as part of the experienced 2nd Infantry.

To the south was the 28th Infantry Division, getting a rest from combat, and the new 9th Armored Division, fresh from arrival at Normandy and not combat-tested.

It was quite a combination of new troops and experienced combat-tested units. All in the slow, low-activity Ghost Front waiting for activation to support the efforts towards the Rhine River.

In August of 1944, when Hitler learned that the Americans had broken out of Normandy, he knew he was in trouble. The German Army was losing against Russia in the east and was starting to lose to the Allies in the west.

During June and July, the Red Army had ripped a hole 100 miles wide and 200 miles deep into Hitler's Army Group Center in the east. The Russian summer offensive annihilated his 9th, 4th, and 3rd Panzer Armies and 500,000 Wehrmacht soldiers.

Germany continued to surrender territory on almost every front. After successfully assaulting the Normandy coast on June 6, British, Canadian, and American armies began pouring onto the European continent. The Western Allies broke clear of their beachheads during July and August and rapidly advanced across France and Belgium. Paris was liberated on August 25, Brussels nine days later, and the port of Antwerp fell on September 4.

By September, Germany was without friends and deserted by its Axis partners. Relationships with them were no help. The Italian government had been overthrown, and the Japanese had fallen back on the defensive. They recommended that Germany start negotiations with Russia for an armistice. Finland broke with Germany while Bulgaria and Romania switched sides and joined Russia.

The German Army had started with ten million troops, and over four million had fallen. An additional 1.2 million soldiers had been lost over the last ninety days, half of them on the Western Front.

These military threats would concern any national leader. Adolf Hitler remained determined, however, even confident in the face of catastrophes on the Eastern and Western Fronts during the first weeks of September. This was partially due to his unbridled optimism and confidence in Germany and its people. Another important factor was his belief in the force of will, notably his own.

The Führer's willpower was sorely tested when assassins detonated a bomb in his East Prussia headquarters, dubbed the Wolfsschanze

Jack's Story | **67**

(Wolf's Lair), shortly after noon on July 20. While the explosion failed to kill Hitler, he sustained significant physical and psychological injuries.

Hitler always suffered from paranoia, which increased after the assassination attempt; henceforth, all his food had to be tasted before he would eat it, and visitors to the Wolf's Lair were searched for hidden weapons before entering.

On September 16th, Hitler finished his daily conference at the Wolf's Lair and asked his trusted generals to join him in his inner conference area. He needed a way to go on the offensive and turn the war around.

General Jodl, second in command of the German Army, mentioned a glimmer of optimism for Hitler. The British and American armies had run out of fuel, creating an Allied logistical crisis. Fall weather had succeeded in grounding much of the Allies' airpower. And Jodl said that many German troops had been getting rest and resupply along the Westwall and in the Ardennes.

Hitler Plans an Ardennes Offensive

The magic word "Ardennes" excited Hitler, and he suddenly announced to his senior military commanders, "I have just made a momentous decision. I shall go over to the counterattack, that is to say." He pointed to the map unrolled on the desk before him: "Here, out of the Ardennes, with the objective Antwerp."

Hitler aimed to divide the British 21st Army Group to the north and the American 12th Army Group to the south, then drive through the seam to capture the vital supply port of Antwerp.

Hitler believed that achieving this goal would compel the Western Allies to accept a peace treaty in the Axis' favor, ending combat on the Western Front and allowing all forces to turn against the Russians in the East.

In 1940, against the advice of his military leaders, Hitler successfully used the Ardennes Forest region to launch a blitzkrieg against France. While Allied attention was diverted to Holland and Belgium, he snuck a giant panzer group through the Ardennes to shatter the French front at a vulnerable spot. This time, he wanted to power through the weak defenses of the Allies' "Ghost Front" and then move northwest to take the Belgian port. Without Antwerp, the Allies would have difficulty resupplying for what Hitler thought would be their final push toward Berlin.

The immediate goal of the attack was to reach the Meuse River within two days. In 1940 the timetable had been accomplished, but that was in May, not December. This would bring them a clear path with good roads to capture Antwerp before the Allies were in a defensive position to stop them.

Hitler conceived this operation, dictated its time, place, and objective, and later involved himself in virtually every detail of its execution. The two most essential issues for success in the planning were the internal security of the plan and being able to deceive the Allies and make them believe that its objective was the defense of the Rhine River.

Hitler had the power of the death penalty over secrecy violations, and even the well-disciplined, high-ranking officers of the Wehrmacht seemed to have been apprehensive of the personal risks each encountered during the planning.

To maintain the security of the plan and deceive the Allies, Hitler named the plan "Operation Wacht am Rhein" (Watch on the Rhine). The name made German commanders accept "as gospel" that the massing of material and the withdrawal of divisions from the front was intended to provide a fresh reserve for the defense of the Ruhr Valley.

Hitler ordered a strategic concentration of troops east of Aachen around Cologne as part of his deception plan. This feigned counteroffensive would be paraded before the Allies. The "cover plan" was propagated to German commanders on the Western Front and retailed to the Allies through neutrals and double agents.

While the Allies watched German activity in the Rhine River Valley, German troops and equipment, under the greatest secrecy, were quietly being moved into the Eifel behind the thin line manned by the weak

German Seventh Army. The Fifth Panzer Army was moved into place, and the Sixth SS Panzer Army was quietly moved from Cologne at the last moment under darkness to its position, ready for the attack on the morning of December 16th.

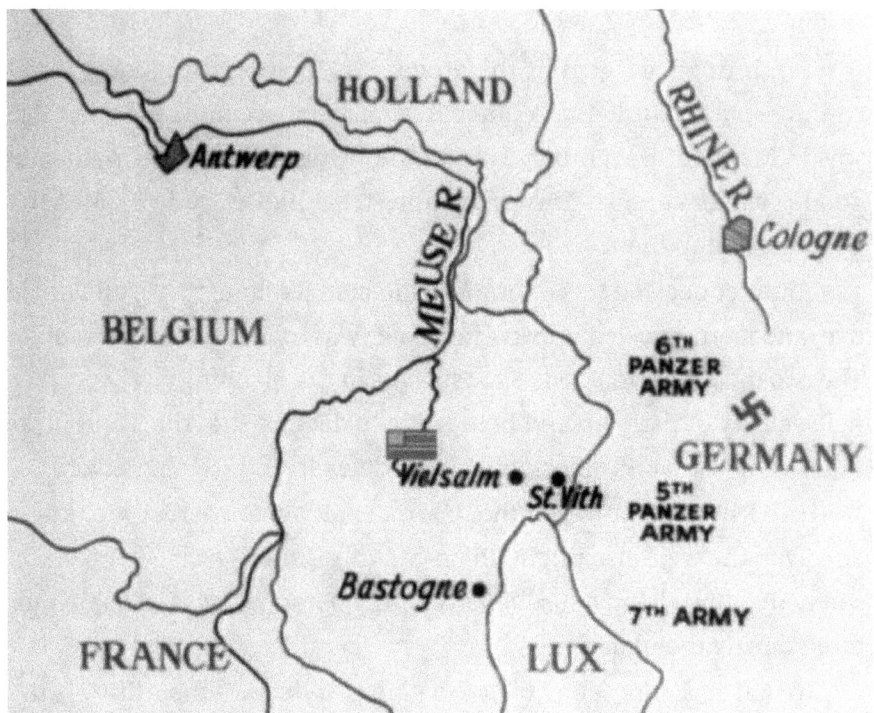

CHAPTER EIGHT
German Attack

Soldiers of the Reich! This day, you are to take part in an offensive of such importance that the whole future of the war may depend on its outcome.
—Adolf Hitler

Hitler's deception plan worked perfectly; he gained total surprise.

At 5:30 a.m. on Saturday morning, December 16, 1944, the first explosions startled and awoke the American 106th Infantry Division, only a few days after it had arrived on an icy ridge in the Ardennes Forest called the Schnee Eifel.

Three German field armies comprising twenty-eight divisions, including nine Panzer divisions, attacked the thinly defended "Ghost Front" sector of the American lines in the Ardennes.

The Americans were thrown into chaos along the whole front. Major General Troy Middleton, the VIII Corp commander in Bastogne, didn't realize the extent of the attack until the next morning, December 17th. One intelligence officer remarked on the first day that it was "just a local diversion."

Once the attack began, radio communications on the Ghost Front rapidly broke down. Little information filtered to either VIII Corps headquarters or the 106th Infantry headquarters in St. Vith as the offensive continued.

Chaos ruled the day. The total surprise the Nazis sought to inflict was complete and devastating. The Americans were unaware of the enemy's intentions and overwhelmed by the size of the attack. Higher command had no idea that at that stage of the war the Germans were even capable of such an offensive. This was such a sudden turn of events that reports back and forth between units and various headquarters were confused and uncertain at best.

During those first hours, each division and units within divisions made decisions and took action independently. Some fought as hard as possible as the Germans attacked and surrounded various units. In contrast, some withdrew to take up better defensive positions and continue to fight, while others just ran from the enemy, clogging the roads to the rear.

This chaos rose to all levels of command as no one knew what was happening, and commanders remained unaware that it was a full-on German invasion with a gigantic number of troops and tanks committed to battle.

The Germans were attacking simultaneously all along the 80-mile front.

Joseph "Sepp" Dietrich's Sixth SS Panzer Army was attacking in the most northern area, between Monschau, Germany and Manderfeld, Belgium. His mission was to cross the Meuse within two days and make an open run to the vast Allied supply base at Liege, then onward to the port of Antwerp. This was to be accomplished by:

First, four infantry divisions and a parachute division would be sent on an attack to open a hole in the American lines. This would allow the I SS Panzer Corps a path to the Meuse River below Liege.

Second, send the 12th SS Panzer Division north to secure the vital Elsenborn Ridge, the northernmost battle in what would eventually be known as the Battle of the Bulge.

Third, propel the 1st SS Panzer Division straight for the Meuse. To ensure speed it would be led by an independent battle group that could seize bridges, towns, and fuel dumps, with the rest of the division following in support. Once a breach was made in the US front, follow-up divisions, both infantry and panzer, would pour through to the Meuse.

The attack started at 5:30 a.m. on December 16th; it began with a massive 90-minute artillery barrage using 1,600 artillery pieces.

As planned, the Germans got the terrible weather they expected, grounding Allied aircraft. However, the bad weather also proved troublesome to the attackers, resulting in appalling road conditions.

Poor traffic control caused jams that delayed fuel deliveries to the front lines. This stalled the main I SS Panzer Corps thrust through the gap between the Elsenborn Ridge and the Schnee Eifel, two strategically important locations in the battle. Elsenborn Ridge offered a vantage point for artillery, and the Schnee Eifel was a natural barrier that could be used for defense. The delay caused them to veer south to start west again toward the Meuse River.

Moreover, the 12th SS Panzer (Hitler Youth) Division's effort to capture Elsenborn Ridge was stopped cold by the hard fighting of the 99th and 2nd US Infantry Divisions.

Hasso von Manteuffel, a wiser and sounder military tactician than Dietrich, grouped his Fifth Panzer Army on the left so that his tanks would be in the fray for the first assaults. His attack was in the central area to capture and secure the two critical road junctions of St. Vith and Bastogne to open the way west toward the Meuse. His initial attack at 5:30 followed a light artillery preparation.

The Fifth Panzer Army fared better in the center Schnee Eifel sector, with a marked numerical and material superiority over the thinly spread US 28th and 106th divisions.

Two infantry divisions of Manteuffel's LXVI Corps surrounded the Schnee Eifel containing the 422nd and 423rd Regiments of the green, inexperienced "Golden Lions" of the US 106th Infantry, perched atop this small segment of the Siegfried Line.

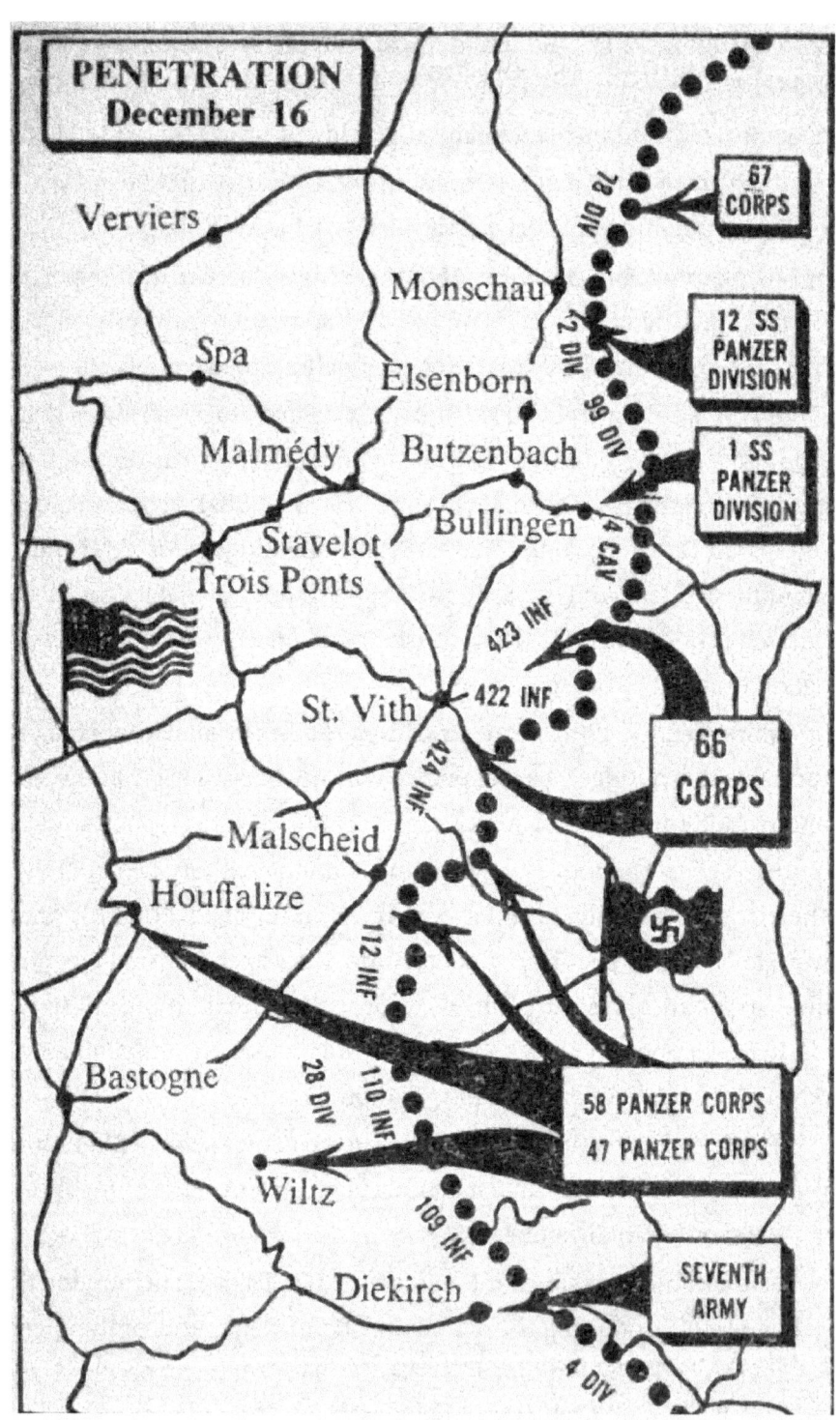

They were left to fend for themselves without support from their headquarters in St. Vith. After a few days, the Germans forced the surrender of 7,000 men, who were marched to POW camps. This was the largest surrender of American troops in the European Theater (in the Pacific exceeded only by the 1941 US surrender at Bataan).

Two German corps with two divisions were to burst through the 28th Infantry Division and isolate Bastogne. The 28th, which had sustained heavy casualties in the Hürtgen Forest during First Army's drive to the Roer River, fought doggedly in place using all available personnel and threw off the German timetable, delaying their movement to the Meuse.

The mission of General Eric Brandenberger's Seventh German Army in the south was to push back the US 4th Division, which had just entered the Ghost Front for rest after fighting in the Hürtgen, the series of battles fought from 19 September to 16 December that chewed up so many formations, the longest US battle on German ground during World War II.

After handling the 4th Division, Seventh Army was to move forces rapidly west and establish a defensive line from Echtemach to Givet on the Meuse River. They would defend that line against any Allied forces coming from the south.

Although the 4th Division's lines were dented, the GIs in that sector managed to hold the Germans. The Seventh was the weakest of the German armies, with no panzer divisions, and was primarily meant to form a defensive shoulder on the flank of the main offensive.

Meanwhile, not knowing the extent of the German attacks, US VIII Corps requested armor support to back up the 106th Infantry Division on the front line. General Bradley and the 12th Army Group staff met on the afternoon of December 16th to tentatively select an armored division to reinforce the VIII Corps in the Ardennes sector. The choice in the north fell on the 7th Armored Division under General Hasbrouck's command.

Jack's Story | **75**

Late in the evening of December 16, Middleton obtained the release of the 7th Armored Division from Ninth Army reserve for rapid movement to St. Vith to assist the 106th Infantry under Major General Alan Jones in his already grave situation.

Jack's 17th Tank Battalion was informed at 8:00 p.m. that it would start its road march at 9:00 the following morning. Jack and his commanding officer, Stan Nizinski, began organizing the platoons for the morning departure.

CHAPTER NINE

The Battle of the Bulge

The Road to St. Vith

Upon getting orders to move south, General Robert Hasbrouck requested travel routes and schedules. He was to send an advance party to Bastogne that evening and the full Lucky Seventh as soon as possible.

Can you imagine if you had to coordinate over 1,500 vehicles, including tanks, trucks, ambulances, vans, and jeeps, along with 11,000 troops from Greenwich, Connecticut, across the George Washington Bridge from New York City and down the New Jersey Turnpike, on two-lane roads, in the dead of winter during rush hour?

Now let's think about doing this in 1944, with a war going on, and everyone needing to use the same route south. The Ninth Army controlled the northern road network. The First Army held the southern road network. Control of the road network and scheduling is complicated, with each Army command having traffic regulators to issue clearances and assign routes.

General Hasbrouck was delighted to have these routes assigned by 7:00 p.m. on 16 December.

Hasbrouck directed Brigadier General Bruce C. Clarke and some staff to report to Major General Middleton of VIII Corps at his headquarters in Bastogne, Belgium. "Find out what is going on and call me."

Clarke was on the road by 8:00 p.m. and arrived in Bastogne at four in the morning.

Middleton told Clarke he wanted to have the 7th Armored to back up and support the 106th Infantry Division in St. Vith. Then he suggested Clarke get a few hours of sleep before driving back up to meet with General Alan Jones, commander of the 106th Infantry Division. Clarke radioed Hasbrouck to tell him that the division's destination would be St. Vith, not Bastogne. He also suggested that the division assemble at Vielsalm, a few miles west of St. Vith.

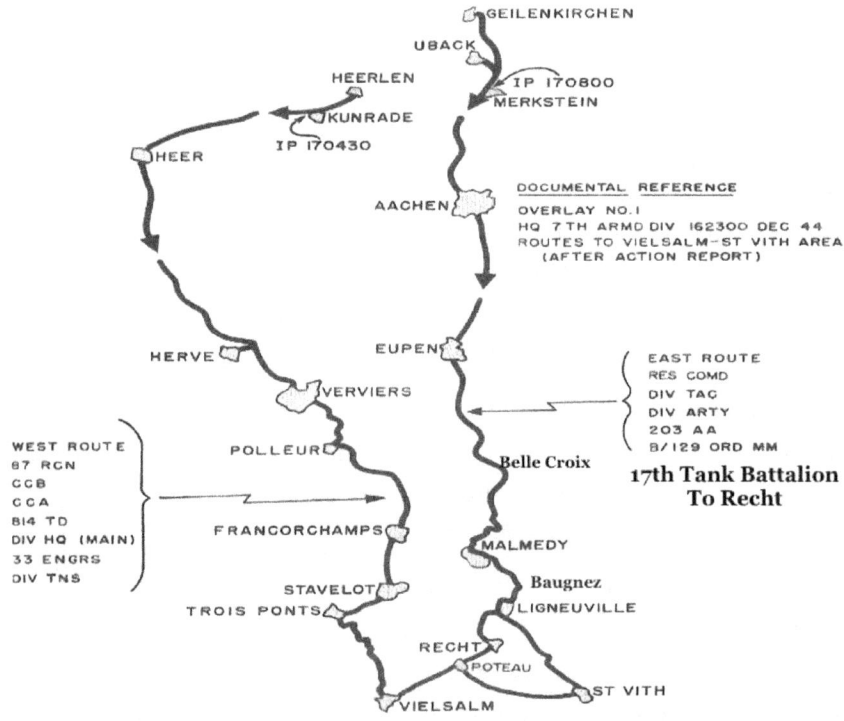

The 17th Tank Battalion continued its preparation to get underway at 9:00 in the morning. Their route would take them south along Highway N62 through Herzogenrath, Aachen, Eupen, Belle Croix, Malmedy, and Lignenville, into an assembly area just south of Recht, six miles north of St. Vith.

Jack and the battalion's other company officers were informed of a German breakthrough somewhere south. Still, the extent of the penetration and the battalion's exact mission was unknown.

Why was there so much confusion and lack of information?

Middleton still did not fully understand the gravity of the situation in St. Vith, nor did he relate the urgency. He did not know how the road network was managed or how long it would take to move the division; however, he believed the move could be made overnight with the fresh armored division available in St. Vith by 7:00 a.m. on December 17th. They arrived later in the afternoon.

The troops formed at the assembly point for their morning departure. There was little sleep to be had as everyone was getting their units ready. Jack talked about his platoon sleeping in their tanks. The weather was cold and bitter, and the insides of the tanks and half-tracks had no heat; the hard metal of the vehicles sucked all the heat from those inside.

The Lucky Seventh was scheduled to travel on two roads south. Most took the west road to Vielsalm, while the rest took the east road south to Recht.

On the morning of December 17th, Company A was behind the Headquarters Company of the 17th Tank Battalion. As the 1st Platoon leader, Jack followed directly behind Major Tom Dailey, the 17th's second in command. Dailey led the eastern road column, taking the lead while commander Lt. Colonel Wemple moved around the battalion in his jeep to ensure all was well.

Hitler's Plan to Stop Support from the North

An essential part of Hitler's plan was to successfully stop any movement of British or American reinforcements, such as the 7th Armored, to the south during the first 48 hours to interrupt Germany's drive to the Meuse River. Hitler named the effort "Operation Stossel." This required a night-time parachute drop of elite troops on December 15th just north of Malmedy to take and hold a significant roadblock at Belle Croix. The mission was to hold the roadblock until Sepp Dietrich's 12th SS Panzer Division relieved them after 24 hours.

This would be the Germans' first and only night jump in the war. Lt. Colonel von der Heydte, a highly decorated commander of the Reich's most elite parachute unit, was assigned to run Operation Stossel on December 8th, giving him only seven days to prepare for the jump.

He received no further instruction but was told that he could not use his entire paratroop group for fear its activation would alert the Allies. He was allowed 800 men, 100 each from eight different paratroop units.

Intrigue and politics played a disastrous role in the planning and execution of the jump. It was rumored that von der Heydte was loosely connected to the ring of officers who sought to bring down Hitler on July 20th, 1944. Heydte felt he was under scrutiny, and an investigation into his possible involvement with the assassination attempt on Hitler was underway.

Colonel Claus von Stauffenberg, Lt. Col. Heydte's cousin, had been a chief architect of the plot not just to take Hitler's life but to persuade the top military echelon to throw in with the coup once Hitler was dead. Stauffenberg planted the bomb under the table just before the conference room at the Wolf's Lair exploded; although four people were killed and almost all survivors were injured, as we know, Hitler was only slightly wounded.

Over 200 officers were convicted in "Show Trials" and executed. The purge continued, and over 20,000 Germans were ultimately killed or sent to concentration camps.

Military heads decided not to trust von der Heydte based on the rumors, but the jump, as Hitler demanded, would occur. The various Nazi commands lost sight of the purpose of the jump or wanted it to fail. Rather than elite troops, he was given a bunch of misfits and troublemakers. After the war, Heydte expressed his feelings: "Never in my entire career had I been in command of a unit with less fighting spirit."

Additional men from his regiment went against orders and followed him but their presence made little difference.

The paratroopers and pilots required much training, which was impossible with only a few days before the jump. The Luftwaffe would not commit to supplying aircraft for the December 15 drop, but only 24 hours later for the 16th. A request for aerial surveillance of the drop zone was rejected – insanity for a night drop.

With minimal combat experience, the 112 aircraft, which carried 1,000 men and 300 straw dummies, took to the dark skies through a blizzard, with no visibility and heavy winds, on their way to Belle Croix, Belgium. They were scheduled to hit the drop zone at 3:00 a.m., allowing time to set up a roadblock and stop the 7th Armored Division on its route to St. Vith.

The pilots' incompetence was stunning. At least 250 men with containers of radios, heavy weapons, and supplies were dropped around Bonn, Germany, 48 miles from the drop zone.

Only a few planes made it to the drop zone. The side winds were 35 miles per hour, causing the death of over 200 as they jumped and were crushed against trees and other obstacles. Many more were immobilized with severe injuries. Other planes returned and landed with all troops still on board.

Von der Heydte personally made it to the landing zone, and collected 125 soldiers that first day. However, without any way to communicate and no arms or other supplies, it was impossible to carry out the mission. He hid in the woods, waiting to cross back over to German lines. Only 80 men survived the operation. Von der Heydte made it to the German town of Monschau, which was in American hands, and surrendered.

The lack of support represented by certain Nazis to sabotage the jump caused one German publication to call it "Operation Murder."

Hitler's plan failed. The 7th Armored Division passed Belle Croix during the middle of the day without encountering German resistance, and Dietrich's 12th SS Panzer Division failed to overcome the American

99th and 2nd Infantry Divisions. It would not have been able to relieve the paratroopers in any case.

Even though the mission failed, the many small groups scattered from Bonn to Belle Croix meant reports of enemy paratroopers were coming in from all over; the Allies thought the German jump behind their lines to be much larger than it was. The Allies committed a combat command of 300 tanks and 5,000 troops for several days to locate a large force that was never there.

The Malmedy Massacre

As they traveled through Malmedy, hospital workers cheered for the American column. Somewhere outside the town, Battery B of the 285th Field Artillery Observation Battalion, a column of about 30 vehicles and roughly 140 men, had stopped earlier, falling in line behind the 17th Tank Battalion going south. The 285th was not part of the Lucky Seventh. It had been part of VII Corp in Aachen, Germany, and was assigned to join Middleton's VIII Corps in St. Vith.

Jack, with the 17th, had just passed through the crossroad at Baugnez, Belgium, halfway between Malmedy and Ligneuville. A short time later, the lead battlegroup of the 1st SS Panzer Division, the Leibstandarte (Bodyguard) Adolf Hitler, entered the crossroads from the east.

SS Obersturmbahnführer (Lt. Colonel) Joachim Peiper had been delayed in his effort to reach the Meuse River within two days. Destroyed bridges, land mines, and jammed roads had caused the SS to continually change their route, even as they created havoc wherever they went.

Peiper had a reputation as a heartless tank commander and was considered by Hitler to be among the elite. His troops in Ukraine had murdered many civilians and Russian troops in a wave of terror and fright no human should have to endure. The Western Front would be no different.

Much has been written about the Malmedy Massacre, though sadly there are few firsthand accounts. Fortunately, the National World War

II Museum in New Orleans was able to conduct an oral interview with a survivor, Ted Paluch, who served with the 285th.

Ted was a draftee from Philadelphia and had just finished with his battalion fighting in the Hürtgen Forest. As Ted explains it:

"We were in the Hürtgen for a while; that was a bitch I'll tell you. The damn trees would explode from the German artillery, and in just a matter of days, it seemed that every tree within sight was stripped bare of all limbs. It was a bloodbath in there." As bad as the Hürtgen was for Paluch, the worst was yet to come.

"The lead vehicles in our convoy were fired on. The lead vehicles were way ahead of us, and the Germans were still a good bit away from them, so when they were fired on, they had a chance to run and get out of there, which they did."

As the lead vehicles sped out of harm's way, the remainder of the column came under fire from the rapidly approaching SS tanks. Ted told what happened next:

"I saw them coming, and our column stopped. I jumped out of the truck and into a ditch full of icy cold water. All I could hear was firing. I popped my head up to see, and all I could see were bullet tracers; I never saw so many tracers in my life. I pulled my head back down as a tank rolled around the corner and approached us. I could see the men in the tank; the troops with them were SS troopers. They had the lightning bolts on their collars. All we had was carbines, and this tank was coming down the road right at us. As it got close, it leveled its gun at the ditch, and the tank commander told us to surrender. What were we going to do? I threw my carbine down and threw my hands up."

Paluch was taken captive by two SS troopers and searched. They then sent him and others to the crossroads and into a field alongside. They were searched again and the Germans took anything they could use. Ted said of his captors:

"I had socks, gloves, cigarettes, and anything of value they took. The guys that captured us were young; they seemed like ok guys. They didn't mishandle or rough us up; they took us prisoner, searched us, and then moved on. They were combat troops and didn't have time to mess with us POWs. The guys that captured us and the tanks with them stayed around for about ten minutes and then disappeared. We were standing in the field with our hands up, not knowing what was coming. I could hear guys praying; maybe I was too…you know…you could hear it, all you could think of was getting away."

As the initial SS troops moved on, the rear echelon infantry came into view and began to pass the large group of American prisoners standing in the open field. Ted continued:

"One of the vehicles came around the corner and started firing into our group. I don't know who the hell it was or why they started firing, but they did. We were standing there with our hands up, and I was in the front of the group nearest the crossroads. As the German tanks passed, they fired into the middle of the group. Everybody started to drop, and I dropped, too. I got hit in the hand as I went down. After that, as each vehicle passed, they fired into the group of us lying there, dead or dying, in the field. Anyone that was moaning, they came around and finished them off. After that, they went back and took off.

"After laying there for, I guess, an hour or more, I heard a voice I recognized yell, 'Let's go!' so I got up and ran down a little road towards a hedgerow. The Germans came out of the house on the corner and took a shot at me, and I dove into a hedgerow. I had some blood on me and laid down in the hedgerow. I heard one of them come running toward where I was lying to look me over; I could feel that guy standing above me. He could have shot me in the back and gotten it over with, but he didn't. I knew he was waiting for me to move, but I just laid there...dead still."

Ted lay in the hedgerow and later stuck his head up. Not seeing anyone, he rolled off along the ground and crawled along a railroad line that happened to take him into Malmedy. Ted continues:

"Along the way, I met some other guys from my unit who had survived. We all came into Malmedy that night together."

While in Malmedy, Paluch's wound was tended to, intelligence interrogated him, and within two weeks, he was back with the remnants of the 285th – back in action in the Ardennes.

On the Road to Recht

Word of the massacre spread far and wide in the sector. The Malmedy Massacre incensed the Americans fighting in this area as few other atrocities had managed to do. Security was tightened at each roadblock.

American MPs stopped the 17th Battalion at a roadblock with explosive devices across the road. Major Dailey explained that the column behind him was headed for Recht.

He was questioned extensively about items only an American would know. Passwords didn't matter. He was asked about the Brooklyn Dodgers. They wanted to know the manager's name (Leo Durocher), and then his wife's name. Dailey laughed about the Dodgers, as he was an avid fan. Once satisfied, the MPs let them through.

The road into Recht was very busy with traffic coming from the south, and military equipment was abandoned along the route as units were trying to escape the advancing Nazi tanks and infantry. The 17th Tank Battalion established a headquarters just outside the town.

The 17th had barely settled into its assembly area at Recht when an alarming report arrived – the Germans had swiftly occupied Ligneuville, less than five miles to the north, a mere 30 minutes after the Americans had passed through the town.

The formation took shape just south of a railroad and underpass to the southeast on the Recht-Wieschen road. The supply trucks, vital for the operations, were on this road, and two were in the town; tragically, these two were lost, and others to the south suffered the same fate. Three trucks were lost in Recht. Four members of a recon party had been left at the bridge at Ligneuville; two were cut off, and two went missing. At this time, there was no infantry with the tanks.

As the 7th Armored Division took up positions in and around St. Vith, it thought the area was safely under the control of Middleton's VIII Corps and the 106th Infantry Division. Instead, the unit confronted a ferocious enemy and retreating, panicked American forces.

St. Vith and its vital road and rail center would fall to the Germans unless the Lucky Seventh intervened.

CHAPTER TEN

Defending St. Vith

A study of Hitler's Ardennes Offensive allows us to finally appreciate the efforts of individuals and small teams that went into the Battle of the Bulge with little or no direction from or communication with higher command. For several days, they were cut off and surrounded by German troops. They didn't know how large the offensive was nor what the German mission entailed. The simply had to stand and fight.

Jack Wilson was just one of the 8,000 men belonging to or attached to the 7th Armored Division at St. Vith from December 17–23, 1944. For six days, they fought against a German force of 87,000 troops, including 20,000 support personnel, enjoying a ten-to-one advantage over the Americans.

German morale on December 17th was extremely high. All units were proud and delighted with smashing through the 80-mile Ghost Front those first 24 hours. The Nazis displayed a passionate determination that they could not be stopped. Most troops displayed skill and initiative, indicating the presence of veterans – or at least veteran leadership – after fighting for several years on the Eastern Front against Russia. This was the best concentration of divisions that Germany had put on a Western battlefield since 1940.

St. Vith was situated on a low hill surrounded by higher hills that were excellent positions to defend the town of several thousand. It was the hub of the best road network in the northern part of the Ardennes Forest, including major roads in all directions and a large freight depot with rail tracks that converged from north, south, east, and west. Germany needed to control it, and the 7th Armored had to defend it at all costs.

Confusion ruled the day, as there was little communication between any units and little knowledge of what was going on with the greater German advance. The commander of Combat Command B (CCB) of the 7th Armored Division, Brig. General Bruce Clarke, was directed to defend the St. Vith road network from the northwest village of Recht extending southeast and around St. Vith from the advancing Germans.

The Battle for Recht

The 17th Tank Battalion deployed its four tank companies south of Recht. Each platoon determined its best position to cover the area where it could place commanding fire on the town and west along the road from Recht to Poteau to block German incursions. The 17th generally fought in support of one of the division's armored infantry battalions but was without infantry in Recht.

Jack describes the situation: "German advances surrounded our units at once, and we were cut off from friendly troops for six days. Each night, Company 1st Sgt. Robert Johnson singlehandedly took a half-track vehicle through the German lines, got cigarettes and ammunition, and returned."

The 17th Tank Battalion was positioned to cover the 7th's northwest flank. While the Germans' initial attack was successful in gaining the town of Recht, the 17th's strong stand caused the Nazis to become so disorganized that they were unable to exploit their gain until they had regrouped after daylight, giving the 7th more time to prepare for the attacks that were to follow.

The Germans were surprised by the tenacity of the American forces. They spent much time trying to find weaknesses in the American defense by poking and jabbing at places around St. Vith, with Recht as a priority sitting on the road the Germans needed to get to the Meuse River.

Recht was a small village five miles northwest of St. Vith. The Germans had two major routes for armor that appeared on their operation maps. The northern route ran through Recht, and the southern one was five miles south of St. Vith and ran through Burg Reuland. The importance of the St. Vith road network was three-fold: to ensure the isolation of the 106th Infantry Division troops that might be trapped in the Schnee Eifel 12 miles south of St. Vith; to cover the German supply columns that were following the enemy armor; and to feed in reinforcements using the St. Vith road network.

The main east to west road ran through the center of Recht, with some raised train tracks and an embankment in Jack's platoon's line of fire.

At first the 17th Tank Battalion had no idea about the hornet's nest they had entered, nor that a German invasion was coming directly at them. At 2:00 a.m., the Germans launched the first of many bitter attacks that would be hurled at the 7th Armored Division for six days. Jack and his platoon were alerted by small arms fire and enemy vehicles moving in the area. C and D Companies covered the underpass all night, while Jack's 1st Platoon was west of the main road.

The attacks increased as mortar, machine gun, and small arms fire were coming from the town. German tanks started moving in, shooting flares to silhouette the American tanks. Heavy tank losses were inevitable without infantry protection. C Company killed numerous German infantrymen attempting to close with their panzerfausts, a single-shot light anti-tank weapon similar to a bazooka. Throughout the night, sporadic shooting could be heard.

As dawn broke, the tanks picked out their targets and began firing. At around 9:30 a.m., December 18th, an enemy tank appeared over an embankment with only its gun visible and opened fire, hitting two American tanks. One was lost, while the other had its gun put out of action but could still withdraw. Jack recalls that this moment was particularly tense, as they were suddenly facing a heavily armed enemy firing at them from a position of strength.

The Americans returned fire on the enemy tank and forced it to pull back. At noon, two maintenance men were sent to the earlier knocked-out tank to secure replacement parts but were driven back by small-arms fire. Shortly after, the enemy tank withdrew, and an assault gun tried to force the underpass. Sgt. Clem Piontkowski, Jack's senior NCO, worked his tank into position and fired into the underpass, forcing the assault gun to withdraw. Two German members of the gun crew were injured.

Later, Jack pulled his 1st Platoon back several hundred feet, and the 2nd Platoon was withdrawn to a nearby location. The 3rd Platoon formed a roadblock. Throughout the day, the tanks fired on enemy positions from these locations. Sgt. Peterson's tank destroyed several enemy vehicles at the crossroads, while other tanks threw 15 rounds into a building presumed to be an enemy command post. About 40 Nazi soldiers ran out; later, ambulances carried the wounded away.

The American tanks spotted many enemy tanks in the valley to the west. They were a little out of range for effective firing (2,000 to 2,500 yards), and their fire was frequently withheld for fear of giving away their positions and running out of ammunition. The units believed themselves cut off and wished to make every shot count.

Finally, one infantry platoon moved forward Monday evening and dug in along the ridge south of the embankment. At midnight, an enemy patrol infiltrated the American infantry and approached Sgt. Piontkowski's tank. It was second from the left in the 1st Platoon's line. The patrol reached within five yards of the tank before Piontkowski realized they were Germans; he opened fire, killed two, and saw patrol members drag off a third man who was either killed or wounded.

At the time, the enemy units that had attacked Recht were not identified. By nightfall, they had revealed themselves as the 1st SS Panzergrenadier Regiment of the 1st SS Panzer Division. This was Adolf Hitler's Leibstandarte: vigorous, well-trained, in splendid physical condition, and superbly equipped.

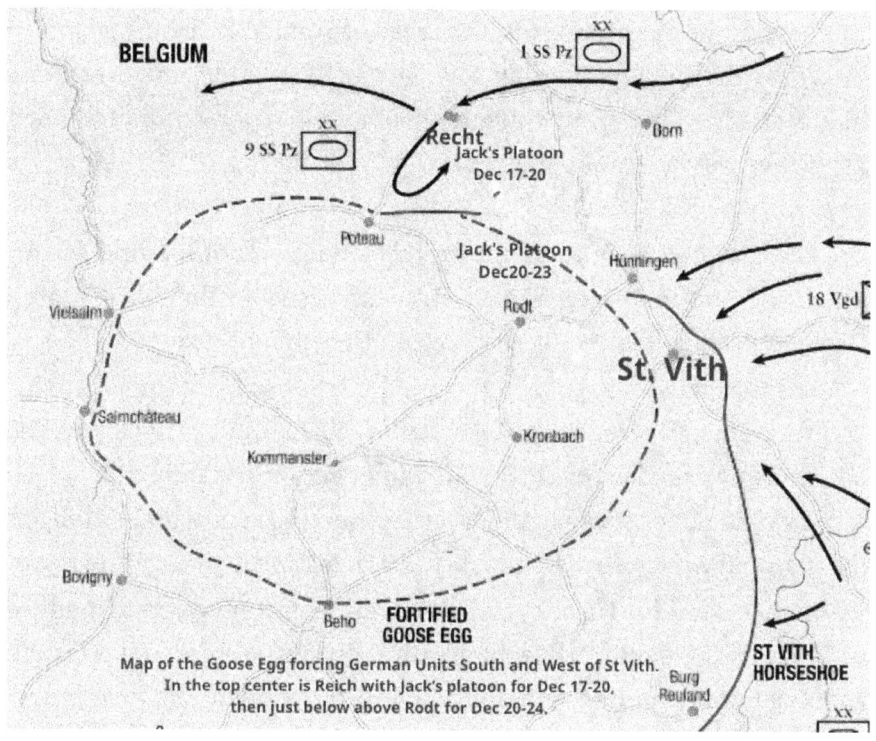

Map of the Goose Egg forcing German Units South and West of St Vith. In the top center is Reich with Jack's platoon for Dec 17-20, then just below above Rodt for Dec 20-24.

Having taken Recht, the Germans pushed out to the southwest and captured Poteau in the morning. Jack and the other tankers counted seven Nazi tanks along the southwest road. The range was over 2,500 yards so the Americans could not effectively engage. Other American units were brought in to retake Poteau and secure the road, while the 17th Tank Battalion continued to secure the crossroads around Recht.

By the evening of December 18, the 7th Armored Division had formed a ring around three sides of St. Vith, described as a "horseshoe" or a large "goose egg." This became a strategic landscape to force the Germans east, south, and west around the St. Vith defenses, protecting valuable road and railroad intersections.

As the battle surrounding Recht raged on, the fighting grew more intense. On Tuesday, the 19th, Jack and his fellow soldiers faced a new threat – an enemy sniper who had taken up residence in a house nearby. Several rounds were fired at the house to take out the sniper, and after that, no more shots were heard from the house.

Despite the daunting odds, the tanks continued to fire on targets in the valley throughout Tuesday. The fighting was fierce, and every shot mattered. The American soldiers, displaying unwavering resilience, knew they were outnumbered and outgunned but steadfastly refused to give up.

The 17th had been in Recht for three days, cut off behind enemy lines, and had not received communications from the 7th Armored Division headquarters since arriving on December 17th.

The Germans were so closed in on the 17th's armor companies that Lt. Col. Wemple shared with Major Dailey, his Executive Officer, that he felt it was time to destroy their codes and encryption equipment so the Nazis would not capture it. Major Dailey convinced him that as long as the material was close at hand, they could destroy it quickly if overrun.

As night fell on Tuesday, artillery concentrations were called for and laid on the center of Recht and the southern crossroads. Despite running low on ammunition, they demonstrated their resourcefulness as trucks finally managed to get through. This was reassuring for the troops as they continued the fight.

Throughout the night, vehicles were heard going through the town, and there was some small-arms fire, but no enemy patrols were seen. There was mortar fire on the units and burp gun fire from the embankment. They were on high alert, ready to fight off any threat that came their way.

On Wednesday morning, the 20th, the battalion received orders to withdraw from Recht. The movement began between 9:00 and 10 a.m. To screen the withdrawal, the valley floor was smoked. They traveled down the main St. Vith road, still under American control, to Ober-Emmels. Jack with Company A and a platoon of D Company light tanks pulled off the road, and the other units passed on their way to help support the southern and western portions of the "horseshoe" protecting St. Vith.

Company A and the light tanks were assigned to the 87th Cavalry Reconnaissance Squadron under Colonel Vincent Boylan.

CHAPTER ELEVEN

The Führer Escort Brigade Takes St. Vith

Hasso von Manteuffel, commander of the German 5th Panzer Army, was responsible for taking St. Vith. He believed it could have been done on December 17th, allowing the Germans to easily make it to the Meuse River below Liege, Belgium, cross it, and be on their way to Antwerp. He became angry as the German attack failed to puncture this hastily organized defensive belt; his timetable had met its first serious setback.

Recognizing that due to the tenacious American opposition his troops could not capture the essential road network of St. Vith, von Manteuffel summoned up his reserve, the crack Führer Escort Brigade (Führerbegleitbrigade), headed by General Major Otto Remer, one of Hitler's favorite generals. Manteuffel ordered this elite armored unit to move north of St. Vith to slice off the base of the "horseshoe" at Recht and then clear out the American defenders at St. Vith and Rodt.

In the meantime, Manteuffel, with his eyes on the distant Meuse River, moved the bulk of his panzer divisions south and westward around the 7th's "horseshoe" defense, leaving the 18th and 62nd Volksgrenadier Infantry Divisions the job of capturing St. Vith with the support of the Führer Escort Brigade after taking Recht.

The earlier retreat of units of the 106th Infantry Division and other units after the German attacks on December 16th left the route almost impassible with discarded, blown-up equipment and other debris along the side of the narrow roads into St. Vith and those north as far as Malmedy. The narrow roads caused tanks and heavy equipment to travel single file in any direction.

With the roads jammed and the strength of the 7th Armored protecting the St. Vith area inside the defensive "horseshoe," the Führer Escort Brigade took three days to maneuver into position.

By December 20th, everything was ready for Remer as he poked and jabbed at the Americans along their eastern defense. The 18th and 62nd Volksgrenadier Divisions were positioned to launch a coordinated frontal assault on St. Vith.

Generals Hasbrouck of the 7th Armored and Jones of the 106th Division watched uneasily while German panzer units moved south of them outside the defensive "horseshoe." They were blind to what the Nazis were doing without intelligence from Army headquarters. They could not develop or communicate cohesive plans, and it was not clear whether reinforcements would be sent.

This left junior officers commanding small units, such as platoons, to make decisive decisions with little command support or ammunition. These local American defenders of St. Vith anxiously watched the German movements. The defenders were on edge the entire time, working with other local units to support each other. At the same time, the Germans poked all around them, testing their ability to defend their respective areas.

After being detached from the 17th Tank Battalion at Ober-Emmels, Jack's Company A (A/17) and the light tanks from D Company were under the command of Captain Harlan Stine, of Company F of the 87th Cavalry Reconnaissance Squadron, which, like the 17th Tank Battalion, was part of the 7th Armored Division. Captain Stine had a full plate, commanding his task force and utilizing these five new platoons.

A crucial defensive position was 600 yards from the town of Rodt, on a rise 100 feet above two important roads. One road went two miles northeast to Ober-Emmels, and the other passed through the town of Huntheim to St. Vith, three miles east. Stine gave A/17 responsibility for this position.

Stine sent his 2nd Platoon of F Troop up the road to Ober-Emmels with a few light tanks to outpost for A/17 and observe any enemy movements on the north-south road connecting Recht to St. Vith.

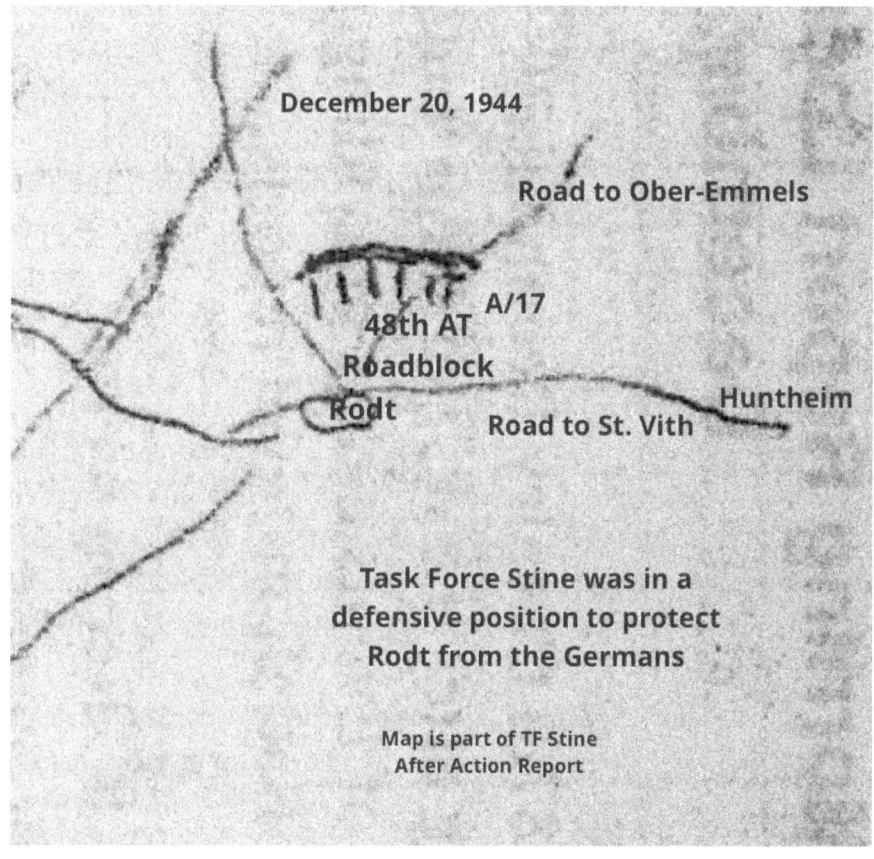

Just below the position Company A had established, the 48th Armored Infantry Battalion's Anti-Tank Platoon was manning a roadblock to protect Rodt. Stine took an infantry platoon and the four tanks of D/17 and positioned them to connect A/17 and the 48th. His infantry was dug in along the crest of the hill with the light tanks to their rear in support.

Jack's Story | **95**

Jack set up his 1st Platoon, placing two GIs as lookouts in front of each tank. They spent the afternoon monitoring any activity on the two roads. About sunset, the recon platoon at Ober-Emmels radioed that German tanks were approaching. The light tanks were forced to pull out when enemy heavies entered the town. The light Stuarts returned and joined Jack's platoon without their infantry support.

The infantry was supposed to maintain contact with Lt. Wilson but failed, so Jack had to contact the 31st Tank Battalion for infantry support. Jack and Sgt. Martin started for the 31st and ran into a tank that could not be identified in the dark. It failed to respond to their hail, so they backed out.

Later, they resumed the trip and found that the tank had moved on. It may have been a German tank, but they were not sure. The 38th Armored Infantry Battalion didn't have any spare infantry. Running patrols over a wide gap with only two supporting tanks was necessary. One tank was pulled back to throw flanking fire on anything coming over the ridge.

On Thursday morning, December 21st, Jack obtained two tanks from the 87th Cavalry. Since there was no infantry to outpost them, Jack returned to the 38th and got his infantrymen back. One tank was moved just above the road from Huntheim to Rodt, and two light tanks guarded the left of the road. Patrolling GIs of the 38th Battalion did fine work, except for two sergeants who took off that night and were never seen again.

The 3rd Platoon of A/17 pulled back over the hill when the Germans began firing 88mm high-explosive (HE) and then armor-piercing (AP) shells at the unit. Things were getting hotter all the time. Unit members tried to observe where the enemy fire was coming from. The shelling was from Otto Remer's Führer Escort Brigade, which was now moving toward Rodt to capture the village.

Thursday night was quiet until the artillery cut in. Then anti-aircraft opened up with 20mm and 50-caliber fire. Burp guns could be heard, and it was obvious that the Germans were attacking up the road.

Earlier, F Troop's 2nd Platoon had opened fire on enemy units, killing and wounding many. American artillery was concentrated on Ober-Emmels and was believed to have done significant damage. The 2nd Platoon met an attack coming across a field and held its position. In the 3rd Platoon sector, German infantry started across the woods and the platoon fired on them, causing a retreat.

General Remer's troops took St. Vith and then Rodt on Thursday night. The 7th Armored Division's "horseshoe" defense was being collapsed into a smaller "Fortified Goose Egg."

General Hasbrouck, commander of the 7th Armored, had learned that all units on the north side of the German offensive had been put under British 21st Army Group command, reporting to British Field Marshal Montgomery. Units to the south were kept under Omar Bradley's 12th Army Group command. As the Germans captured St. Vith and Rodt, General Clarke of Combat Command B, 7th Armored had lost almost half his men and equipment to the Germans. Resupply of CCB was virtually impossible.

Hasbrouck requested orders to withdraw all his units to Vielsalm while there was still an opportunity to move beyond the newly arrived 82nd Airborne to safety. He told them he would continue to fight the advancing Germans if necessary; however, if there was no way to withdraw, it would be the end of the 7th Armored Division.

Field Marshal Montgomery approved the withdrawal and put Colonel Boylan of the 87th Calvary in charge of the units east of Rodt for withdrawal, including Jack's platoon and the rest of Company A of the 17th Tank Battalion.

CHAPTER TWELVE

"Fight Your Way Out"

Withdrawal from the "Goose Egg"

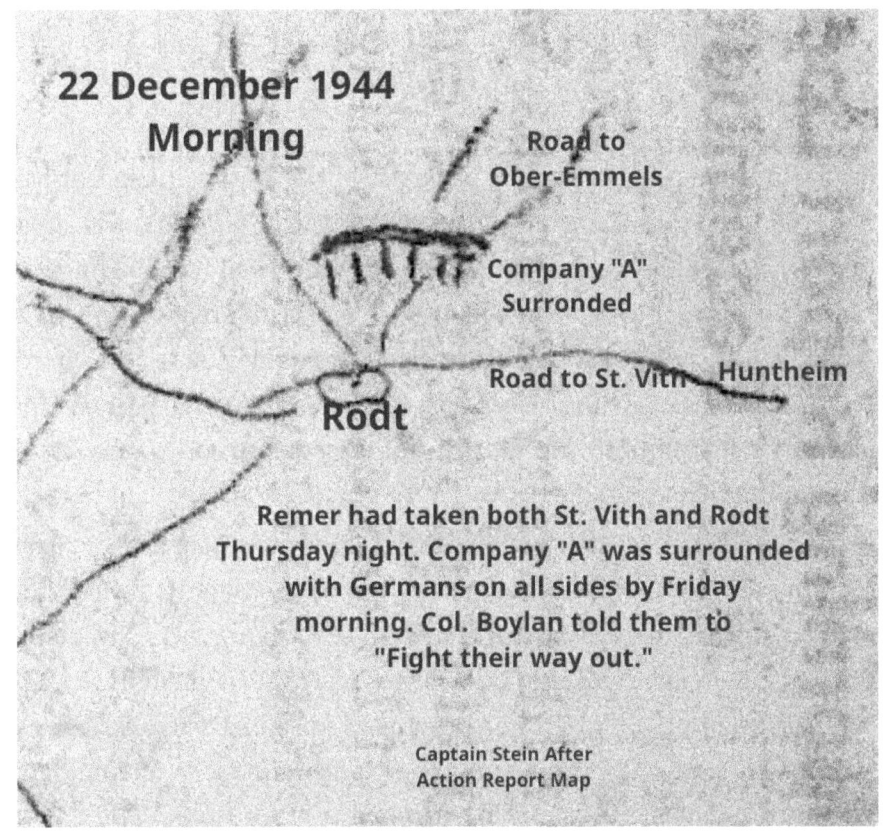

Captain Stein After Action Report Map

Around Jack's unit it was quiet until around 9:00 p.m. Thursday when the distant sounds of artillery fire were heard in Ober-Emmels to the north of their position. The tankers were still on a hill 600 yards northeast of Rodt, which gave them views of the road from St. Vith through Huntheim into Rodt and the road from Ober-Emmels to Rodt. The tanks and equipment were all positioned below the crest of the hill and out of view of traffic on the two roads.

As the night progressed, the sound of firefights got closer. It was only later that Company A found out the Germans had taken both St. Vith and Rodt that night, putting them directly behind the German lines and blocking their path to withdraw west to Vielsam, where the 7th had established a HQ behind the 82nd Airborne Division, protecting the bridge to safety across the Salm River.

There was little sleep as the outpost GIs and forward observers watched the enemy traffic flowing into Rodt on both roads. They were all part of Remer's Führer Escort Brigade.

Company A was now attached to British Second Army. Jack said: "We were told to hold the Germans at all costs." But when the British learned of our situation, Col. Boylan of the 87th Cavalry "ordered us to fight our way out." While the American high command had been inclined to hold at all costs, as at Bastogne, the British took a different view in their sector, as Field Marshal Montgomery decided to "tidy up the battlefield." This meant tactical withdrawals from endangered points of the front in order to build up a strong force to fully contain the enemy, then counterattack.

The embattled elements of the 7th Armored pulled out at about 9:00 a.m. The tanks were assembled 1,000 yards northeast of Rodt. The 2nd Platoon had pulled up to assemble when it saw enemy tanks advancing from both their front and rear. Lt. Williams had to abandon his tank, and Sgt. Sturtevant's tank, which had been partly disabled, was also left. As the group assembled, German units were on all the roads surrounding them.

Company A and stragglers from other units were waiting for the command to move out when Lt. Stan Nizinski asked all the tank commanders and other NCOs to meet so he could brief them on the situation.

He informed them that he was going to surrender the group to the Germans to save as many lives as possible. The group made several comments, none supportive of the lieutenant.

Jack believed that the Nazis did not take tankers prisoner. Rather, they killed them. He thought about the lieutenant's decision and concluded that surrender was not an option.

Lt. Jack Wilson pulled his M1911 .45 auto pistol on Lt. Nizinski, arrested him, and took command of the company.

In late January 1945, Jack's parents received a letter from his friend Bill Bacon's parents telling them about the incident.

> We at home here call him a hero. We had a letter from Bill on Monday, written on January 25th. He said a lieutenant in Jack's Company told him that Jack had been made Commanding Officer of the Company. The lieutenant told Bill the story of how it happened.
>
> Their unit was in a rugged corner behind German lines, and the commanding officer wanted to surrender the Company to the Germans. Jack told him if he made one move to leave his tank, "I should turn every piece of artillery in the tank on you." Then, Jack took command and got them out of their tight spot. He was made CO of his Company.

The Withdrawal Begins

The tanks lined up on the road with 20 infantrymen hanging on each tank. They had eleven tanks along with other vehicles in a single file with Jack's tank leading. The road was so narrow that only one tank at a time could advance. They moved southwest towards the rail tracks at Neundorf, St. Vith. The tank column ran into hundreds of advancing German infantry without knowing what was happening. Jack said, "The

Germans were shocked at seeing our tanks, causing rifles and overcoats to be thrown in the air as some tried to surrender and others ran to their rear."

It was foggy, and hard to see what was what. Men were seen, but it was hard to tell whether they were enemies or Americans, so fire was withheld.

The tanks started cross-country, and anti-tank fire took out one of Sgt. Piontkowski's tracks as it moved out. The ground was boggy, and Jack's tank got bogged down and had to be abandoned as the Germans directed armor-piercing 88mm shells and machine-gun fire. When Jack exited his tank, he signaled the others to go on. Sgt. Saunders soon had to abandon his tank, and Sgt. Wolfe's tank was hit, making a loss of four tanks.

Jack and his crew boarded a 48th Infantry half-track with a couple dozen other men. It went for half a mile and then turned over in a ditch; nobody was injured. The men proceeded on foot, picking up guns on the way. Jack took command of the first of the remaining tanks. The column continued west between Hinderhausen and Crombach.

At about 3:00 p.m., three 87th Cavalry tanks came down the road from Rodt. One was hit by fire from an unknown source and abandoned at 4:30. The other two pulled in beside a building; Jack's company units withheld fire and were about to send runners to investigate when the two tanks turned around and drove toward Rodt. It was believed that Germans manned them.

Communications with the 87th Calvary were challenging and were usually maintained through the radios in the light tanks. Now the group had no light tanks.

Friday night, the group continued to pick up stragglers, including two understrength infantry platoons and a light weapons section with three mortars and two light machine guns. The group was about 2,000 yards down from Rodt, hearing the diesel noise of German half-tracks and tanks. American medium artillery opened up and is believed to have caused much damage. No patrols were met that night. It was freezing.

On Saturday morning, December 23rd, the enemy took Crombach and infiltrated the unit's rear. The Germans came in from Rodt with panzers, the number of which is unknown. Two US tanks were knocked out, along with one tank destroyer, which had accidentally fired on Jack's tanks. One Sherman wouldn't start and had to be abandoned.

The remaining tanks pulled out on the road south from Rodt to Commanster, where they halted. Three tanks and three tank destroyers were left. One tank destroyer covered the road over which they had come, while one medium tank was moved north of Commanster, where two more Shermans and two tank destroyers joined them.

Two men had been badly burned when the tank destroyer was knocked out. First aid was being given to the other and administered when word came to withdraw further. The unit went to Commanster. There, they found the remainder of the 87th Cavalry's forces. This was between 11:00 and noon.

A stand was made at Commanster when German tanks came up the road from the east. Jack's group lost another tank and tank destroyer, leaving two tank destroyers and two tanks.

The unit retreated west, stopping where a platoon from the 38th Infantry had set up a roadblock. The tanks proceeded back toward Commanster to reconnoiter, and it was found that the Germans had taken the town and set up a roadblock of their own.

It was just getting dark. Only infantry stragglers were available to be outposted. They covered the best they could. That evening the area was pounded by American artillery. Division headquarters could not be reached by radio. Jack's little unit was the only element between the enemy and the division headquarters.

At 8:00 p.m., orders came through to withdraw. The two tanks and two tank destroyers proceeded north to Vielsalm. Another six miles brought the unit to the Salm River, and the bridge was blown after they crossed. Jack's group had been the last American troops to withdraw from the St. Vith salient. They then moved to Trois Ponts, west to Werbomont, north to Harze, and further west to 17th Battalion HQ – now at Liege – arriving at 4:00 Sunday morning, December 24th.

Jack described the withdrawal and Christmas Day:

> Our withdrawal started with eleven tanks and ended with two tanks; we had a small loss of men and picked up over 100 stray GIs en route. It was Christmas Eve, and our dinner was boiled rooster and wine from a local farmer!
>
> The next morning, we observed from our hillside a column of ten US tanks moving across our front from right to left. They wheeled into our front and started firing upon us. We then realized the tanks had been captured and were manned by Germans. They were unfamiliar with the guns, and we decimated them.

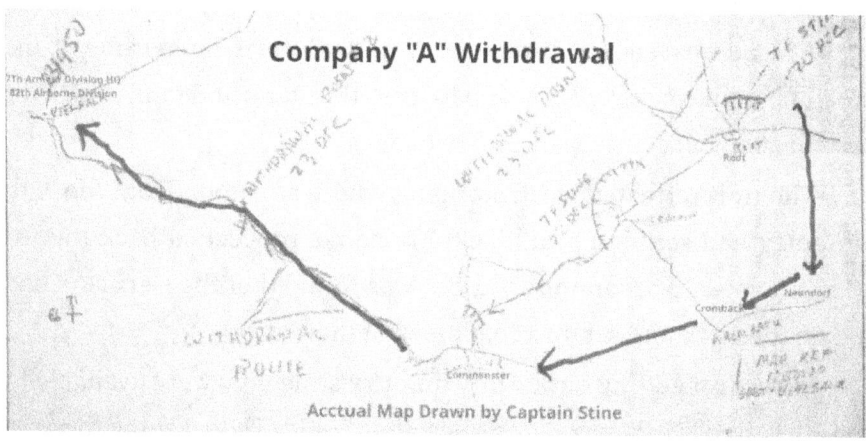

Acctual Map Drawn by Captain Stine

CHAPTER THIRTEEN

The Retaking of St Vith

Training, Training, Training

After withdrawing from the "Goose Egg" on December 24th, Jack's company was pulled from the line to refit. As Jack described, "Our unit was ordered to the rear for regrouping, new equipment, and replacing officers and men. Over the next two weeks, we were issued old tanks from North Africa, cooks, and Air Force ground people to crew them – training, training, training." They were told there were only a few weeks to get the company in shape for active battle.

Interesting information about the Sherman tank pertains to these "older" tanks Jack's company was receiving, which had seen service in the African Theater.

Over the years since World War II, there have been countless debates about the Sherman's inferiority to the German Panther and Tiger tanks. The Sherman was smaller and had less armor. It was designed to support the infantry in battle and not directly confront the German armor. So based on the weight, amount of armor, size of the main gun, and the distance it could fire, it was thought the German tanks were superior.

The German and American requirements were different. The Nazis were fighting a slow and defensive war with fewer tanks. So their tactics, out of necessity, had to be different. Americans wanted to shake loose and fight an offensive war and had the major advantage of 10 times the number of tanks the Germans had. There were few direct tank-to-tank battles, such as ten on ten. There were normally five American tanks on one German, down to two on one.

Mechanically, the Sherman performed superbly, and after groaning and grunting through heavy, sticky mud for weeks on end, it was still sound. If an engine failed, the crew could change it in four hours. The low maintenance requirement allowed it to travel hundreds of miles without mechanical issues. American tactics also differed: the Sherman was not a vehicle built primarily to fight other tanks; rather, its mission, above all others, was to get into the enemy's rear areas, disorganize him, destroy supply and communications, and generally wreak havoc there.

With a large advantage in the number of tanks, American tactics counted on quickly replacing tanks knocked out during combat. For these reasons, the Sherman tank played a large part in ending the war quickly with a minimal loss of tanker lives.

During the two weeks of regrouping, Jack had a chance to catch up with receiving and sending letters. Jack's letters tell much of the story about dealing with his experiences, his excitement over the birth of his son, and his devoted love for Jean. The time involved in getting letters back and forth was generally 20 days each way. It was a long timeframe, however, and much happened in between.

Jack's first combat experience was on November 23, 1944. He couldn't write until the end of November and early December after that combat experience. His letters would not arrive home until around the 15th to 20th of December when he was called into the Battle of the Bulge on December 17th, so he didn't have the opportunity to write again until the end of December.

Letter writing had to become an art. Censorship of correspondence was still a standard that stopped all GIs from telling too much and few were inclined to talk about combat experiences that would cause their families stress and fear for their loved ones' lives. Jack's experience at Rodt, when surrounded by the Germans, where he had to relieve his company commander, was an excellent example of how careful he had to be when writing home about his experiences.

Jack knew the Battle of the Bulge was in all the newspapers at home, along with reports of many killed or wounded. Jean did not know he was even in Belgium; he knew she was smart and would have guessed, however, so he was very concerned.

Having spent what seemed like a lifetime in combat and returning to some sense of normalcy, not seeing the horrors of combat for a while, he longed to be home and have the war behind him. The letters were his only connection to the world he loved and missed.

The letters represent the compression of communication within a short few weeks. Jean would receive some of these letters at the end of January, the first correspondence she had seen from Jack in 40 days.

Jack knew his son would have been born when Jean received his first letter. He told her that he was doing well and had become the tank company commander, and he prayed he would do his best for his men. He had lost all his equipment during the last battles except for the most important thing: the pictures of Jean that he kept in his pocket. The pictures kept him going daily, reminding him how much he loved and cherished her.

As the 7th Armored troops were getting time to relax, it was a great time to blow off some steam, celebrate stopping the Germans, and welcome the coming year. Jack had always loved a party and enjoyed helping to organize it.

They had quite a party on New Year's Eve at the large house where Jack and many officers were housed. Over 200 people attended. A good four-piece French Orchestra entertained while great food was being served, including three roast turkeys, about 25 platters of potato salad, hors d'oeuvres, etc., and two lovely cakes – one a 16-layer job with "Happy New Year 1945" in the frosting. It was a BYOB party, yet to make sure, the group bought two cases of cognac to supplement the festivities, and when the evening ended (breakfast the following day), there was but half a bottle of cognac left!

The house was decorated with evergreens and candles burning in the many cut glass chandeliers, creating a holiday atmosphere. A cartoonist came over and made some reasonably clever color posters for the walls.

It was a big conversation piece over the next few days; even General Hasbrouck expressed his regrets about not coming. He wasn't given an invitation until the last day.

Jack said in a note: "I had a silent toast to you at 12, darling, and I wish you were there in my arms."

Jack had the opportunity to give one man in his company a furlough. He informed Sgt. John Martin, whose brother had been killed in the war a short time ago, that he was being sent home on a 90-day leave. The company thought it would benefit him and his family if he could go home.

Jack said he would never forget the warm expression on his face when he told him. Sgt. Martin would be able to see his baby for the first time. Jack later shared this experience with Jean.

Jack's Son is Born

Finally, on the 4th of January, Jack received a cable Radiogram from Jean's parents, Han and Nell, dated 26 December 1944, telling him of the birth of his son on Christmas Day. Jack was so excited he couldn't wait to write a letter to his wife.

> I just received the radiogram from your parents. Thank you with all my heart and love for my son. I can hardly wait for the details: how much Peter weighs, the color of his eyes, etc.
>
> I am very happy you were well then; I hope you have your strength back by now.
>
> Since the message, I have been on a cloud and am very happy. Please give him a big hug and kiss for me. WOW, what a Christmas present!
>
> PS: I had seven cigars, so I passed them out this morning.

The next evening he wrote about the Radiogram and his fun visit from the Chaplain, Father Czubak:

The Radiogram arrived in the ETO [European Theater of Operations] on December 26th and entered the regular mail system. Due to our location's constant movement, it finally came on January 4th.

You can imagine how excited and thrilled I was with the news. Imagine that you are more than ready for a bit of relaxation.

Tonight, the chaplain, Father Czubak, talked to me and told me that "I was pretty mean to have a baby on Christmas to avoid buying him birthday presents." Father Czubak inquired, "Where did you study engineering?" I replied, "Business Administration major." Fr. Czubak said, "I just received a cable that you have a son born on Christmas day. Pretty good engineering!" We all got a good laugh out of the remark. He is a swell fellow.

During the German Ardennes Offensive, known as the Battle of the Bulge, newspapers back home reported that the Americans were losing the war to the Germans. There are ebbs and flows in any war, and the press had seen nothing but victory since D-Day and the success of pushing Germany out of Holland, France, and Belgium. Jack pointed out how the attitude on the home front affected those fighting. They didn't understand it. "Darling, with all the stories we hear coming from the States, the most popular topic of conversation here is what is wrong with the people at home?"

The truth of what happened was quite different than that reported in the news. Hitler bet his country of Germany, "the whole farm," believing the Allies could not stop him and would capitulate, going home with their heads hanging down! The Allies only had to stop him from getting to the Meuse River, and they did this by slowing the Germans at St. Vith and Bastogne. Only German recon units from the 2nd Panzer Division managed to reach the Meuse, while the offensive as a whole ground to a bloody halt. It was the final turning point in the war. There were still many hard battles to fight, but Germany was now back on its heels as it had to defend its homeland from the Allies in the west and the Soviets in the east. Jack wrote:

> Your latest letter is dated Tuesday evening, 12 December. I now have it before me, and I drink in deeply each beautiful word you penned.
>
> My dearest Jeanne, I pray you don't worry too much about me here. Indeed, a man has a certain amount of fear when he goes into combat, but one must exert his self-control at such a time and exercise those fears to make one keener and react more quickly in a given situation.
>
> Also, the idea I've been a commander, whether of a tank, a platoon, or a company, gives you added responsibilities so that whatever inhibitions and fears come upon you, they must be subordinated to your duties. I have found, as others have also, that our faith in God has given us that strength that is sometimes necessary.

The soldiers' tough mindset about their situation demonstrates what this generation was about: "The glass was more than half full." Not sharing their stress in writing was recognized as an opportunity to share their secret thoughts when Jack finally got home with Jean and Peter.

Positioning for the Return to St. Vith

The 17th Tank Battalion, including Jack's Company A, moved east about eight miles north of Malmedy to the village of Halt. The 7th Armored Division was putting the various units in assembly areas as it worked on the plan to retake St. Vith from the Germans.

Jack and his company settled in; they were training for their mission. This would take back the last of the territory the Nazis had acquired in the Ardennes Offensive, placing them in a defensive position as the Allies continued to mass more troops against the original incursion.

The weather had been terrible: Jack thought it was "colder than blazes here, and I couldn't keep my feet warm. It will be a great day when this whole mess is finished."

He was very pleased with his company's cooperation and professionalism; they had become a good team. The weather was a problem the last night before moving into position. It was not cold enough for the muddy ground to freeze. Adjustments would need to be made to deal with the mud, which would bog down vehicles and equipment.

This would also be the first combat for many of the replacements. He remembered his first day of combat, just two months earlier, on Thanksgiving Day. The calming effect of the combat vets he fought with had settled his nerves going into battle. His Company A had many who had fought from France through Holland to the Battle of the Bulge, and their experience would give the same comfort to the new combatants. They were all well-trained and highly competent in doing their assigned jobs.

The next day, Jack was heartbroken to hear that Chaplain Father Czubak, who had shared the news of Peter's birth, was killed in the town of Diedenberg by German artillery while assisting a wounded soldier. He had developed such a warm relationship with Jack.

January 22, 1945

The 7th Armored Division's defense at St. Vith, Belgium, from 17 to 23 December 1944, had split Hitler's Ardennes offensive, stopping the Germans from reaching the Meuse River, where the Germans planned to split the British and American forces and take Antwerp. This turned out to be Germany's last major strategic offensive of the war.

The final push to recapture St Vith would kick off on 23 January. Jack's part in this battle actually began the day before.

On the morning of January 22nd, Lt. Colonel Wemple, the 17th Tank Battalion's commander, formed Task Force (TF) Wemple to capture two German-held villages, Am Stein and Diedenberg.

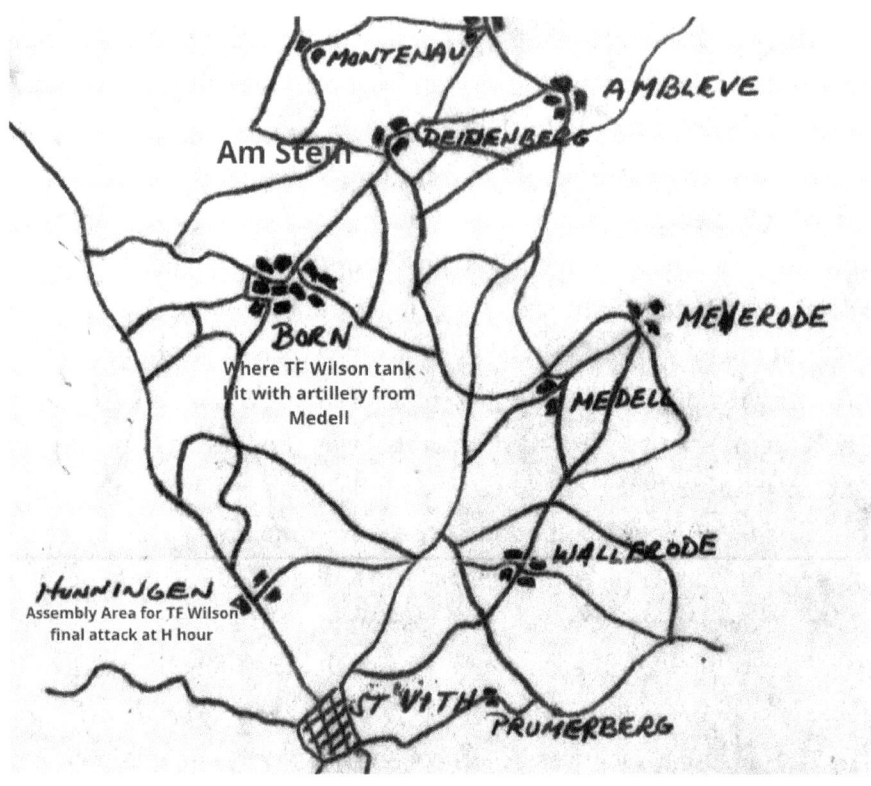

Jack, the commander of Company A, was selected to command TF Wilson, and Captain Britton was to command TF Britton. Captain Britton was the commander of Company B of the 23rd Armored Infantry Battalion. Each task force was assigned a village, and TF Wemple would be in overall command.

Jack's task force comprised two tank platoons (five tanks in each), one infantry platoon, an engineering platoon, and an anti-tank platoon. They moved forward and were positioned to attack. The 7th Armored HQ wanted to change positions before the attack, but Colonel Wemple countered by keeping them in place.

Wemple ordered Britton's task force to attack as planned. At first TF Wilson was ordered to stay in place because Britton's force, to his right, had not advanced as fast as expected.

Finally Jack was ordered to move his group south and cross the Emmels River near the village of Montenau. He was then to attack and secure the high ground north of the village of Am Stein. Jack was to move with infantry mounted on his tanks until enemy resistance was encountered. The GIs would then dismount and fight through with the support of the tanks. Artillery shelled the buildings near Am Stein before Jack's force moved out at 9:30 a.m.

Jack's task force advanced 600 yards north of Am Stein, while Britton's was just north of Diedenberg. Britton received some light small-arms fire from Diedenberg and a few rounds of anti-tank fire from his left flank. As they passed, tankers and infantry were conducting reconnaissance by fire at the potential enemy positions. By 11:30, TF Britton was in the town of Diedenberg and had taken four POWs as the GIs went house to house to clear the village. Britton's force suffered no casualties.

As Jack's Task Force Wilson approached Am Stein, they received anti-tank and small-arms fire from their right flank. It was coming from the high ground just north of the village. Jack called in a concentration of artillery fire on the German position and then proceeded with the assault. By 2:00, both task forces had captured 30 additional prisoners. Britton occupied the town of Diedenberg while Jack's group continued the attack on Am Stein.

As they were sweeping the homes in the village, Jack's group was receiving distant anti-tank fire from the vicinity of Born, a little over a mile southeast, so he shifted his force further to the left. Jack's group had cleared the whole village of Germans. The two task forces had completed their missions and captured 54 POWs.

The lack of decent communication between various units had made the mission more difficult. The maps were hand-drawn from a large 50,000-to-1 map. The snow that had fallen over the last several days covered the landmarks, so a simple compass was the key to knowing where you were.

Final Attack on St. Vith

The next day, January 23rd, would see the decisive event when the 7th Armored Division retook St. Vith.

Task Force Wemple was again using TF Britton and TF Wilson to execute the 17th Tank Battalion's requirements, strategy, and maneuvers in the battle. The assault guns, mortars, and tank destroyers were to take up positions in the forward assembly area to support the operation. The light tanks and a small infantry force were to be held in reserve in the forward assembly position to be used as and when needed.

At 8:30 a.m., TF Wemple moved out of the Diedenberg assembly area with mounted infantry on the tanks. The order of march was Britton's group, Wilson's group, the tank destroyers, the Task Force commander and staff, the assault guns, the light tanks, the mortars, and the engineers.

The roads were small trails, and the snow turned to mud, making them impassable for wheeled vehicles. Command ordered all wheeled vehicles, half-tracks, mortar, anti-tank, and engineering platoons to remain in Diedenberg.

When the head of Jack's Task Force reached a point several miles southeast of Born, it received several heavy enemy artillery barrages from the vicinity of Medell over a mile to the east. One of Jack's tanks received a direct hit, killing four of the tank crew and seriously wounding the other member; several infantrymen were critically injured. As soon as Wemple saw how accurate the German artillery fire was, he led the remainder of the force further to the west and kept them in a defiladed position. There were no more injuries from artillery fire.

Wilson and Britton continued the next two miles to the assembly point in Hunningen for the attack on St. Vith. As they arrived, they received some anti-tank fire from the outskirts of the town. 7th Armored tanks and tank destroyers returned the fire and knocked out two enemy SP assault guns and one Mark IV tank.

Moving into position, they saw seven towed German 88mm guns, which the enemy had abandoned. With the guns was a good supply of ammo. The 88's, with one exception, were in good working order. They were not in firing positions but had just been lined up along the edge of the woods and abandoned.

The American assault guns and light tanks had difficulty crossing the railroad and stream. Captain Simon and his battalion maintenance section came forward and assisted them with a small Bailey Bridge, though this delayed the deployment.

The field artillery forward observers and their air support officers were in position with the forward elements and ready to add support when needed.

The combined Task Forces of Wilson and Britton were ordered to remain in position until ordered to attack. Just before 4:00, the forward observers reported three enemy tanks and several dismounted men withdrawing from Hunningen toward St. Vith.

Shortly after this, heavy enemy artillery concentrated on the assault assembly position, and approximately eight infantrymen and three tankers were injured. Lt. Jack Wilson, commanding Company A, received shrapnel wounds in his left arm but refused to be evacuated. He continued to lead his company in the attack. The other injured men were carried back on two light tanks, transferred to wheeled vehicles, and taken to an aid station.

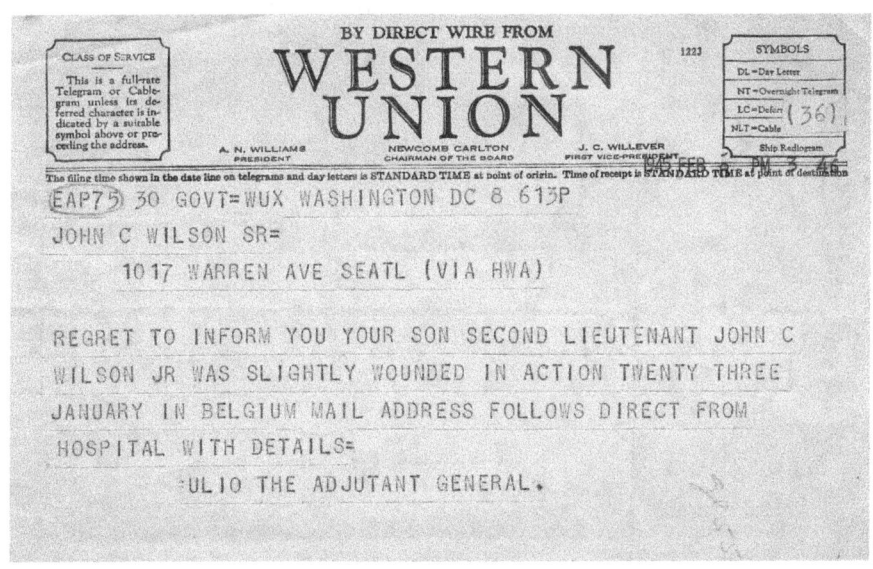

Jack's 1995 Recollections

The time of the initial assault was delayed while engineers constructed Bailey bridges for tank movement. I was the company commander, and at H-hour (the time to move out) minus 30, I had all officers assembled behind my tank discussing the attack. As heavy German artillery arrived, all my officers tried to scramble under the tank for protection. I turned to the right, where a captured 88mm gun was located a few feet away, and dove behind it for protection. An incoming shell exploded, and I was wounded through my snowsuit and combat jacket. I was able to get up and finish the discussion about the attack.

I mounted my tank at H-hour and led the company into the attack. We fought successfully for five hours and returned to the assembly area. After dark, I turned the command over to my executive officer and walked two kilometers to the aid station. Bodies were stacked like cordwood outside the aid station.

After aid, I was sent to the rear to an Evacuation Hospital for surgery. The operating room was a school gymnasium with over 50 operating teams. I was transferred to the 203rd General Hospital near Versailles, 240 miles southwest. (The 203rd had been activated at Ft. Lewis, Washington; many were from the University of Washington.)

7th Armored Takes St. Vith

Tanks, Joes Win Vital Road Hub

By Russell Jones
Stars and Stripes Staff Writer

WITH FIRST ARMY, Jan. 23—St. Vith, the Germans' last stronghold of any consequence on the First Army's sector of what once was a bulging, were recaptured today by the Seventh Arm'd. Div.

Tanks and armored infantry, from 1,000 yards into the key road hub early in the afternoon. After a house-to-house battle which lasted three hours and 10 minutes, the forces under Brig. Gen. Bruce C. Clark, of Syracuse, N.Y., had cleared it of the enemy.

Meanwhile the 75th Div. Inf. Brigade and Mackinaw was fighting toward St. Alertness, three and one-half miles southwest of St. Vith. The 75th Inf. Div. moved 3,500 yards to points southwest of St. Vith.

Planes Blast Vehicles

Ninth TAC flew 400 sorties today against an estimated 1,000 enemy vehicles, after having a record day yesterday along the road north of Prum to Bonn. It claimed 223 motor transport vehicles destroyed, 174 damaged, 16 armored vehicles destroyed, 12 damaged, 20 railroad cars destroyed, 178 damaged, three locomotives destroyed, one damaged, one four dumps and one ammunition dump destroyed, railroad breaks in 14 spots, one destruction of its gunners while three more were damaged.

Seventh Army's drive started at 9 PM with artillery drive by task forces under Lt. Col. Richard Chapelle of Lafayette, La., coming down the Malmedy-St. Vith road and under Lt. Col. Martin L. Riley, of Chicago, coming from the point of woods 1,500 yards straight north of St. Vith.

The task forces, made up of tanks and armored infantry backed by paratroopers commanded by Lt. Col. Richard T. Seale, of Leavenworth, Kan., pushed into the outskirts of the town in the face of small arms fire from Germans dug-in in the eastern edge and with artillery fire hitting them from the vicinity of Wallerode, 4,000 yards to the east.

Third Clears Its Sector

PARIS, Jan. 23—Third Army forces pushed by the fourteenth advance of the 17th Airborne Div., drove the enemy out of all Belgian territory today between Houffalize and the Luxembourg frontier.

American artillery joined Canadian batteries in blasting Rolling German batteries which thinned the once-packed roads toward Germany. The remainder to the south in Luxembourg was battered by the Third Army. Tanks moved in Diekirch.

In the graveyard of the Ardennes was buried the striking force of three powerful German armies and the hopes of the German High Command of a stalemate in the West.

While the German windfield was rows and bombed the fast flowing and transport were being rushed out to destruction was evident that mounting Allied pressure had made the flight position was of the disputed Losheim corridor.

In Holland, attacking British troops extended their right flank advance two-thirds on Hugenholt road points, and captured Vouisenrood, Laffelt and Schiepmeert as well as a string of four more lands lying between those towns.

In Alsace, powerful French forces continued their attack along the Illinois-Inn-Besain road.

In Again

Last Out, First In — 7th at St. Vith

By a Staff Correspondent

ST. VITH, Jan. 23—The Seventh Armd. Div. was back in town tonight, one month to the day from the night they evacuated it after holding five days—three days longer than they had been ordered to—and knocking the Germans back through so far off schedule that other Fifth Army units were able to get farther more reserves they stopped the thrust.

The last Seventh Armd. outfit to pull out of St. Vith that last night of Dec. 22 was an armored infantry battalion under Lt. Col. Richard G. Chappuis of Lafayette, La. Today Chappuis commanded the task force which spearheaded the attack on the town.

Bitter Fight Going and Coming

The Germans were watching even the Seventh's positions when they evacuated St. Vith and Chappuis had to fight hard to get out. Today, although the Germans are retreating, they had to fight to get back in. The armored infantry and the attack, jumping off from Hünningen, 1,400 yards up the Malmedy-St. Vith road.

When they moved off the road into the fields, west of the town warned to disappear into white clothing which left tracks as they stumbled over the snow. They were the men with the new snow suits. Others wore fatigue clothing in the white grey because their suits were stained with Germans were blasted in the fire heat of battle.

The Infantry moved slowly, quickly briefly to avoid the intermittent screeching of the Nebelwerfers—six-barreled mortars—holding the road leading to the town, the road to the fire of them, and sometimes hitting them. They were armored infantry but often than they were hit by other infantry—plodding toward the enemy with only their weapons to protect them.

Supported by Tanks, Paratroopers

Behind the infantry were the tanks and paratroopers under Lt. Col. Edward J. Betts, of Leavenworth, Kan.

The infantry and the tanks and the paratroopers moved against the town flipping out of sight in the hollows of the rough ground, coming up on the hills going through the woods and finally die, appearing for good into the houses on the edge of St. Vith. And while they moved, the constant roar of artillery and mortars was punctuated by small arms fire, the rapid staccato of German guns breaking through the heavier rattle of the Americans.

The Seventh's armored infantry was in St. Vith again.

CHAPTER FOURTEEN

Recovery and Return to Service

203rd General Hospital

Jack was transferred 240 miles after surgery to the 203rd General Hospital between Versailles and Paris, France. He describes the hospital as being very modern: "Good food, clean sheets, flannel pajamas, etc. – hence very comfortable."

On January 25th, he wrote Jean about his wound:

> Darling, I was slightly wounded on 23 January when an artillery concentration came in on top of us. Excuse the writing, as I've picked up a bit of shrapnel in my right forearm, the meaty part, but no damage to the bone. It was nothing serious, yet they evacuated me. You can imagine where it happened. I was very lucky to get off as easy as I did, and I have never prayed as much in my life as I did when those shells came in. Many were less fortunate.
>
> I was operated on last night, and I feel excellent except for a slightly sore right arm. I should be back to the outfit in a week or so. You will receive a note from the War Department about me being wounded in action, so don't get excited when you receive it. It's nothing serious, really. I spent the evening tonight in the Officers Club drinking scotch and trying to play the piano, so you can see I am OK!

I am enclosing a clipping of something which my Company did. It appeared in Stars and Stripes, and the circumstances differ slightly from the story. It sounds comical, like Abbot and Costello's "Who's on First."

Subject: 88s To: Chaplain

By Russell Jones
Stars and Stripes Staff Writer

NORTH OF ST. VITH, Jan. 22—All the horrors of war are not found in the front lines.

A force of tanks, infantry and TDs moved 1,500 yards through the woods and deep snow today to a point dominating roads into St Vith. As the infantry approached the southern edge of the woods, Lt. Col. John P. Wemple, of Shreveport, La., called headquarters to say:

"Hey, we just captured seven brand new 88s, complete with ammunition. What shall we do with them?"

Maj. Joe Ford, of Philadelphia, the S-3, said:

"Hell, turn the damn things around and use them."

And Wemple replied:

"What am I to use for my tanks and infantry then?"

So the S-3 said:

"Wait a minute, I'll call the division."

The division said:

"What?" You got seven brand new 88s, complete with ammunition? Get them to hell out on the road and we'll be down to get them."

Ford told Wemple about it and Wemple said:

"Get them out on the road? Why in hell do they think the Germans left them there? Because they couldn't get them out any more than we can."

So the S-3 called division again and said:

"He can't get them out on the road. What shall we do?"

And division said:

"Turn them around and use them, of course."

"—," said Ford. "Now I'm back where I started. No — way to get them out on the road and no — crews."

Capt. Richard Stern, of New York, the PW officer, came in and said:

"What? No crews? Hell. I can fix you up. I put those crews in my PW cage last night."

Jack was always very outgoing and quickly made new acquaintances with those he met. His ability to ingratiate himself with others was fun for Jean and himself. If there was a chance to make a deal, he was in. On January 30th Jack wrote:

> I am working on a little deal to get you Chanel #5. I'll let you know how it comes out. Ruth Ann Wilson, a Theta at the University of Washington, is a nurse on our floor, and she is swinging the deal. She is also a swell person and knows many of our old gang that we know from the university. She reminds me very much of Hi Caulkins in many ways [Jean's childhood friend].
>
> Here it is! I never thought I would ask you to do this, but here it goes. Will you see if you can buy some hosiery, Size 9 1/2, 45 gauge, in either cinnamon or rose brown or a color that would go with a Forest Green uniform? I told Ruth Ann that you would be glad to try as they have a tough time getting them here. She will probably send you a money order for them, but I told her not to bother.

Then on February 5th:

> My arrangement with Ruth Ann Wilson came together. Last night, she put down a bottle of Chanel #5 and a larger bottle of Corday's "L'Ardente Nuit," which happened to be prewar stuff, as they haven't made any for four years. Ruth Ann said that they are the best, but you couldn't prove it by me. I'll send the bottles and pack them well so they won't break or evaporate.

Jack shared more information on his injury; they had sewed up the wound on his arm a few days before, and he was going to be released from the hospital on Friday. They were tough on rules, including passes: "These people in the rear forget that a combat man likes to see Paris and enjoy himself occasionally. Also, I am gaining a little of the weight I had lost, which is not good. So you can see that it will be nice to get back in the field where you are your own boss, and you can treat your men like they deserve."

Jack wanted to return to the 17th Tank Battalion and get his old Company back. He found one of the hospital nurses who was going to Paris, so he asked her to question any 7th Armored Division officers she saw to find out if they were from my outfit. She returned and told him Colonel Wemple was in Paris at the Washington Red Cross Officers Club. Jack thought he was a great person and a superb commander. He was from Shreveport, Louisiana, and his nickname was "Rebel."

Tuesday afternoon, Jack went to Paris to see Lt. Colonel Wemple to ask to be returned to the outfit and not go through the replacement system. At any rate, Wemple was out, so he left a note in his room.

A nurse told him somebody was there to see him the next day. It was his cousin from Spokane, Tommy Meenach. He was amazed Tommy found him. He put on some clothes and they took off for a long walk. They spent the afternoon together, having a great conversation about family and how everyone was doing. It was their first time together since a family get-together in 1942. Tommy told Jack he had been looking for someone who knew where he was. He found Colonel Wemple, who told him about Jack leaving a note in his room and where he was at the hospital.

Tommy wrote a letter to Jack's parents a few days later about catching up with him, which details the story.

> Dear John & Esther:
>
> Well, I really have some good news for you. I don't know whether you have heard from your son, but if you haven't, I have in person.
>
> He is fine. I know all about his little mishap and believe me, it was very slight. I am sure that when you received the letter from him telling you about it, you had all kinds of visions of him being marred for life, but he is as good as new now.
>
> I had been given a three-day pass to Paris, and while I was up there, I stopped everybody I saw who had the 7th Armored patch on their shoulder if they knew Jack. At first, I didn't have good luck,

but I finally ran across one officer who told me that Jack's Battalion Commander was also staying in the same hotel as me.

The officer pointed him out to me in the mess hall. I immediately went over and introduced myself to Col. Wemple and started to ask him about Jack. He told me it was coincidental but he had just gotten Jack's note in his room that day. Jack had been at the hotel because he discovered Col. Wemple was also in Paris.

He was to be discharged from the hospital the next day, and Jack wanted to find out if he could return to his outfit without going through the Replacement Depot. I read the note, and Jack told Col. Wemple where he was stationed. It was about a 30-minute ride on the train from Paris. The following day, I took the train to the hospital. You never saw a more surprised person when I walked in on him.

It was by far the most exciting time that I have ever had. We spent the entire afternoon together, discussing everything we had been doing. I hadn't seen him since April 1942.

His most significant interest was how his baby son was. He had received only one letter since Peter had been born. He could hardly wait to return to his outfit because he knew several letters would await him.

We both agreed conclusively that we would much rather be back with our wives than where we were!

There were so many coincidences that allowed this reunion to happen. All I can say is that fate was with us. It wouldn't happen again in a million years. This is really a small world.

I want to assure you that Jack is in fine shape and anxious to get back to his men.

I talked to his Col for quite a while, and he told me that Jack was doing an excellent job and was one of his better junior officers.

I just had to write and tell you the good news. It completed my enjoyable trip to Paris. Please keep the letters coming.

Love to you both,
Tommy

On February 11th, Jack was headed back to his unit. He wrote to his parents and did a short recap of the last month and a half.

> I am writing this from our Division's rear installation while awaiting transportation to my company. The Colonel had me reassigned to the 17th Tank Battalion, and I am returning to active duty today.
>
> A brief review of the past few weeks should clear up some points in your mind. I will start with our pulling back from the Germans before Christmas. We had moved right into the middle of the Bulge in the St. Vith area for several days longer than we were asked. The newspapers gave a full account of that action.
>
> It was rather rugged and meant many days and nights without rest and sleep, but we seemed to thrive on it. We were surrounded more than once. As the first platoon leader, I had to lead our company's assault out of the Bulge. More than once, I really thought, "This is it," but for some reason, Jerry was slightly confused at times, and we did okay.
>
> Just before New Year's Eve, we pulled back and rebuilt ourselves. We had a memorable march to a new position in the Bulge and began operations, which resulted in the "Lucky 7th" taking back Saint Vith. At present, upon entering the town, you are greeted with a large sign bearing the greeting:

YOU ARE NOW ENTERING SAINT VITH COURTESY OF SEVENTH ARMORED DIVISION

Jack returned to his unit and caught up on the mail. He had not had any news before regarding his son's health. He shared this with his parents on February 13, 1945.

> When I arrived, I could go through my mail and packages. It was so good to hear that you and Jean are fine, but I am truly upset about Peter's heart and that thing with his eye.

I know he will be well and strong, and as you say, we are fortunate that medical science is so advanced. I pray that he will outgrow this, and I love Jean so dearly for not keeping it from me. She is genuinely a wonderful wife and mother."

Also, how can I ever repay you both for being so kind to her and doing such swell things like going over and seeing her and sending flowers for me? It means so much to me, especially since I cannot do those things myself.

In my mail was a cute note from Peter and Jean: "Thank you, Papa, for the flowers and signed Mama."

Everybody was quite surprised to see me back so soon. In some ways, it is swell to be back with the outfit, yet in others, it will be rather difficult to go up again. I guess that is all in my mind, though (I keep telling myself).

What was causing Peter's problems?

Jean had contracted a case of German measles when she was first pregnant with Peter after moving home to Spokane from Fort Knox when Jack transferred to Camp Cooke in California.

Unbeknownst to both of them and their doctors, German measles caused both physical and mental abnormalities in the baby – now termed Rubella (CRS), congenital rubella syndrome, which can cause life-long problems.

Medical science started discovering a connection between these birth issues and German measles in the mid-1940s, but did not have a vaccine until 1971.

After retaking St. Vith, the 7th Armored Division and the 17th Tank Battalion spent the rest of January and most of February rebuilding their units and staying in reserve in Belgium. Jack was assigned as a Platoon Leader in his old Company A.

The Battalion continued training, preparing for future movements into Germany. On February 25, 1945, Jack could share exciting news with his parents.

Dear Dad and Mom

Last night at the officers' party, I learned I had been promoted to 1st Lieutenant and awarded the "Silver Star" for gallantry in action. Can you believe that? I was astonished at the "Silver Star," as it is a high award. I still don't know how I got it. My promotion is effective as of 18 February. Things all seem to break at once.

I wish I could tell you the circumstances, but I have not seen the recommendation submitted. The action occurred near Saint Vith, Belgium, when my company captured seven Jerry 88mm anti-tank guns. I was evacuated for my wounds the following day.

Your Loving Son.
Johnny

Silver Star Award

Over 100,000 Silver Stars were awarded to the Army in World War II, 351 of which were Awarded to the 7th Armored Division.

Subject: Award of Silver Star

> By the Direction of the President
>
> Second Lieutenant John C. Wilson, Jr.
>
> For distinguishing himself by gallantry in action on 23 January 1945 in the area of Diedenberg, Belgium.
>
> Although wounded in the initial phase of the attack, 2nd Lt. Wilson remained in command of his Company and led it successfully in seizing its objectives. By staying in the vanguard of his forces, although in great pain, Lt. Wilson prevented the dangerous delay that a shift in command would have caused. His outstanding courage and

able leadership contributed to the success of his unit's operations and are worthy of the highest praise.

The action was recorded in the AAR regarding the event leading to the reward of the Silver Star by order of the commanding general.

Hq 17th Tank Bn, After Action Report, Month of January 1945
23 January 1945

The assault guns and light tanks had difficulty in getting across the railroad and stream in the vicinity of 859925. Captain Simon and his battalion maintenance section came forward and assisted them in getting across the obstacle. By 1408, Task Force Wemple was in position and was ready to attack as ordered. The field arty forward observers and their air support officers were in position with the forward elements and were ready to give support when needed. The Task Force was ordered to remain in position until ordered to attack. At 1558, we observed what was thought to be three enemy tanks and several dismounted men withdrawing from Hunningen toward St. Vith. Shortly after this, we received a rather heavy enemy arty concentration on our assault position, and approximately eight infantrymen and three tankers were injured. Lt Wilson, who commanded company "A" received shrapnel wounds in the left arm but refused to be evacuated. The injured men were carried back on two light tanks because wheel vehicles could not get up to our position.

CHAPTER FIFTEEN

Crossing the Rhine River

The 7th Armored Moves East to the Rhine

Through February 1945 the 7th Armored Division remained in reserve, continuing with equipment replacement, maintenance, and training, which left a lot of time to relax and discuss what was happening back home in the States. There was a lot of talk about the shortage of supplies, new equipment, and repair parts for their tanks. As they were on the front lines dealing with the Nazis, the news that impacted them the most was about the "wildcat" strikes in Detroit that caused these delays.

Jack wrote his parents about the matter:

> Our biggest gripe is reading in the newspapers of 35,000 people on strike in Detroit holding up production on our new tanks and other equipment. They should all be placed in uniform, paid $50 a month, and made to work. I guess they think we are drinking pink tea over here. I wish to hell I could take some of those bastards up to the front. Excuse the harsh language, but it's how we all feel. Don't be surprised if the boys over here clean house when they get home, as they are pretty well peeved at that kind of stuff. That's why we aren't getting what we need to fight with! Too many of these people are interested

only in themselves and their next paycheck while we are fighting so they may continue to live as Americans.

The 17th Tank Battalion remained bivouacked in Hoof, Belgium, preparing its equipment and vehicles for moving out. Orders were relayed for Jack's platoon, along with the rest of Company A, to join Colonel Wemple's Task Force and move out on the 3rd of March to Konzen, Germany, to inspect the road network in the vicinity of Schmidt and Heimbach. This area was southeast of Aachen, leading to the Roer River.

The Rhine River was the last of the great barriers before central Germany. The Allies had collapsed the German resistance at the Siegfried Line, and had managed to cross the Roer and advance through the flooded portions of the Roer Valley after the Nazis destroyed the dams.

The Battalion left Konzen for Odingen, Germany on the Rhine above the town of Remagen. In his 1995 recollections, Jack commented, "As we moved east, we passed Cologne on the Rhine River, a mostly destroyed city from Allied bombings, yet the Cologne Cathedral stood untouched."

The 7th Armored moved up to aid in clearing the enemy from the territory west of the Rhine. There was little enemy resistance between the Roer and the Rhine until reaching the area southwest of Bonn, where stubborn pockets of Germans in Rheinbach and Meckenheim held out in an attempt to keep an escape avenue for German withdrawals across the Rhine.

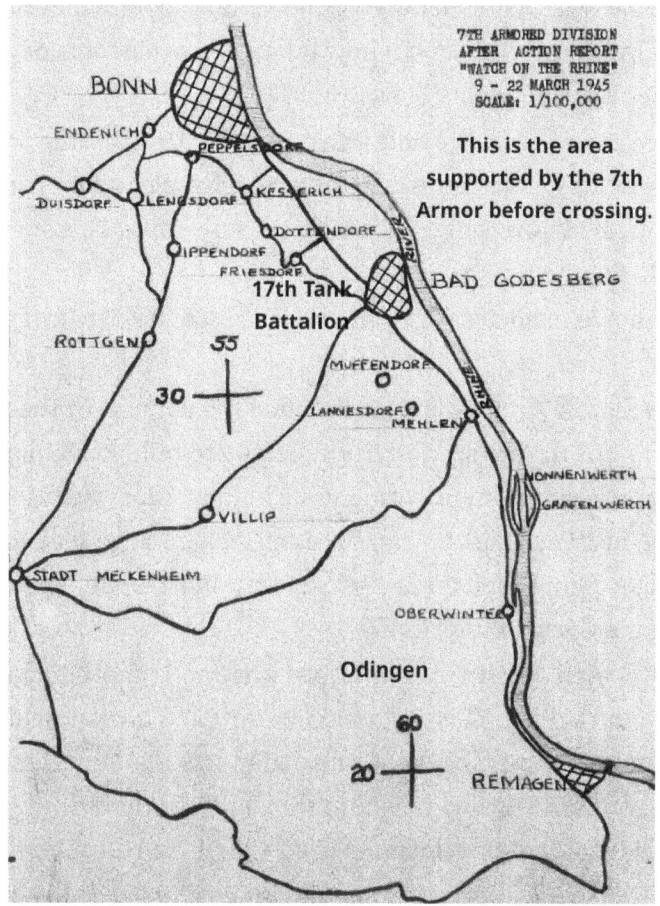

Remagen Bridge Taken

The bridges crossing the Rhine had been blown up by German forces from Cologne to south of Bonn, with the Ludendorff railroad bridge at Remagen the only one still standing. The Germans had wired the bridge with over 6,000 pounds of demolition charges; however, when they went to blow it up, only a portion of the explosives detonated. With incredible bravery, GIs of the 9th Armored Division, not knowing if the bridge would blow up with them on it, ran forward and disabled the remaining charges while bravely fighting their way across and capturing the bridge on March 7th.

After the war, Major General John Leonard, commander of the 9th Armored Division, wrote about how taking the bridge was not planned; sometimes it just happens in war:

"When a reporter at the time asked Sergeant Drabick, the first soldier across the bridge, 'Was the seizing of the bridge planned?' 'I don't know about that; all I know is that we took it,' was his reply. This sums it up in a nutshell. So much for the operation."

Eisenhower said, "It was his best day since the Battle of the Bulge ended."

From March 7th to March 25th, after the capture of the bridge at Remagen, the 7th Armored Division helped to hold it against German counterattacks while engineering units built a Treadway bridge across the Rhine just south of the captured one. The bridgehead across the Rhine was accomplished three weeks earlier than planned, giving earlier access to the German interior.

The Germans used virtually every weapon at their disposal to try to destroy the bridge. This included infantry and armor, field artillery, floating mines, mined boats, a railroad gun, and their giant 540mm super-heavy "Karl Howitzer," whose shots missed the bridge. They also attacked it using newly developed Arado 234B-2 turbojet bombers.

The Germans couldn't destroy the bridge, but it had been unstable since it was captured, partly due to prior American bombing. On March 17th, Combat Engineers were ready to weld a support structure to stabilize the bridge, but as they were working it collapsed into the river. Over two dozen died in the collapse, but a number of engineers had jumped in the river and were pulled to safety at the Treadway.

To protect the other pontoon bridges against aircraft, the Americans positioned the largest concentration of anti-aircraft weapons during World War II, leading to what is believed to be the greatest antiaircraft artillery battle in American history. The Americans counted 367 different German Luftwaffe sorties over the next ten days. The Americans claimed to have shot down nearly 30 percent of the aircraft dispatched against them. The German air offensive failed to sever the bridges, but it did create havoc in the bridgehead and in Remagen itself.

The 7th Armored was deployed along the west bank of the Rhine to support the protection of the bridge. The 203rd AAA Battalion (Anti-Aircraft Artillery) was used to augment the air defense from the constant attempts of the Luftwaffe to take out the crossings.

While awaiting further assignment, the Division occupied the area around Bad Godesburg, a resort and health center on the west bank of the Rhine. The 17th Tank Battalion became responsible for the area, with battalion commander Wemple being made Military Commander of the town and area surrounding Bad Godesburg.

Lt. Col. Wemple's forces established control over the population and combed the area for enemy soldiers who had been unable to escape across the Rhine. Nearly a thousand prisoners were taken during this period – most of them having masqueraded in civilian clothes to escape their ultimate destiny.

The various tank units were deployed at select firing position outposts and within range of 7th Armored artillery support. Any enemy activity was then reported to Lt. Col. Wemple's command post.

With forces starting to cross at Remagen, 7th Armored troops were warned of the advance of friendly formations coming from the south on the east side of the river and instructed to be doubly cautious in observing movement.

On the 12th of March, the 17th Tank Battalion tanks started firing over the Rhine with indirect fire – this meant according to coordinates alone, without a direct line of sight between the gun and its target, as in the case of direct fire.

Jack seldom talked to his children about the war but shared in a 1992 conversation with his grandson, Stephen Wilson: "My only disappointment during the experience at the Rhine was shooting our cannons across the river at the Germans and not being part of the ground combat taking the bridge."

Jack's Story | 133

Adolf Hitler knew that holding the Allies on the west side of the Rhine was paramount to Germany's defense. There was no other significant natural barrier to hold them back. Hitler was becoming more unraveled with the Allies across the Rhine and the Russians at the Oder River in eastern Germany, only 50 miles from Berlin.

Suspecting treachery, Hitler ordered the SS to arrest and try any individuals who were involved with the defense of the bridge at Remagen and have them executed as an example of what would happen to those who failed the Third Reich. To the disgust of his generals, who knew it would cause major moral issues with the troops, the SS did convict and execute many.

Information and Education

Administratively in Washington, DC, the War Department continued to develop programs for the eventual peace. One of the key considerations was how to cater to the educational needs of GIs who were eager to expand their knowledge and skills. Military units at the battalion level had to select officers for specialized training before combat ended.

Lt. Col. Wemple offered Jack the position of Information and Education officer for the 17th Battalion, which he accepted. Jack was to report to school on March 16, 1945, while the 17th continued its mission and crossed the Rhine River into the Ruhr industrial region. After I&E school, Jack would rejoin the 17th.

After hostilities ceased, he would set up a school, appoint instructors, and teach accounting, English, math, practical mechanical work, and other skills to men awaiting the trip home, to the CBI (China, Burma, India Theater), or in occupation duties. Jack commented, "It will be quite a job, but the most challenging." He laughed, "I must attend a 10-day school in Paris next week. [Wemple] told me he knew I was the most qualified officer in the battalion for the position, and I was pretty flattered."

The I&E Division's mission was to improve the quality of training and offer educational opportunities to expand soldiers' horizons and so serve them well in peacetime. The school in Paris was to inform officers like Jack of the services available and how to structure them locally.

The program was established in partnership with the University of Wisconsin at Madison in April 1942 to provide advanced educational opportunities to GIs. They could choose from over seven hundred courses listed in the *What Would You Like to Learn* catalog, and an elaborate range of high school and college correspondence courses was also developed as part of the same initiative. Over one million GIs took correspondence courses in subjects ranging from basic mathematics, automotive repair, and shorthand to American history and the sciences.

The Information and Education classes were taught at the University of Paris, which Jack described as a really nice institution. The courses were interesting and concentrated on post-war educational programs in the ETO for troops awaiting shipment home or in the Army of Occupation. He met many fascinating people and felt it was much like returning to the University of Washington.

He also had fun being entertained by the lovely people from the 203rd Hospital, and he laughed about the "hard duty" those stationed in Paris had to deal with. The subways, however, were his pet peeve with people kicking, shoving, pushing, jamming, and packing themselves in so tight, it was like they were breathing in unison. And then there was the lovely scent of garlic – there was always someone with a peculiar affinity for garlic! "Give me the open field," he wrote, "fresh air, etc., any day."

7th Armored Crosses the Rhine

While Jack was finishing I&E school, the 17th Tank Battalion crossed the Rhine on Treadway and Bailey bridges and assembled south at Reidenbruch. The 7th was back in action as a "classic armor division for which it was designed," as the division historian described. It was launched as the center spearhead for the First Army front, breaking out of the Remagen bridgehead and driving for five days until told to stop.

On the first day of the attack, March 27th, they fought the Nazis for access to the autobahn going south to Limburg. Artillery blasted the defenders, allowing Combat Command R and Combat Command A access to the highway and its subsidiary roads. Both Combat Commands could travel at high speeds, knocking out German resistance. When they came to an interchange, CCR forces went north, and CCA moved east.

On the second day, the progress was remarkable, as columns reached and crossed the Dill River. They had plowed through vast countryside full of two retreating German divisions. Catching the enemy formations from behind, they left hundreds of mangled vehicles smashed and littering the roadside. Thousands of Germans surrendered and were left for the following American infantry to process.

Giessen was captured on the third day, an important railroad center far east of the Dill River. The fight was bitter but short, with hundreds of anti-aircraft Flak guns turned into ground weapons. The 7th rolled through town, and the Flak guns were smashed in piles. On the way to Kassel, the autobahn was full of German troops retreating east; Combat Command A struck near it and left a large number of dead and prisoners behind. Jack rejoined the 17th Tank Battalion in Giessen.

Jack's return coincided with the new orders for the 7th Armored to secure and protect the dam over the Eder River from being blown up by the Germans to flood the Eder Valley, 80 miles north of Frankfurt.

The dam had been breached in May 1943 by bouncing bombs dropped by British Lancaster bombers of the RAF's 617 Squadron as part of Operation Chastise. (This action was immortalized in a 1955 movie, "The Dam Busters.") However, the dam had been repaired in a few months using slave labor.

On March 30th, Jack was part of the Task Force under Major Dailey of the 17th Tank Battalion, which was put in position to repel any German counterattack against Combat Command B. The division destroyed German resistance to reach and capture the great Edersee Dam intact. By nightfall, CCB troops were occupying the enormous lake's southern bank. Outpost positions were established north of the dam itself across the lake.

The Edersee Dam, holding back one of the greatest water capacities in Europe, became a 7th Armored Division prize. The enormous structure, measuring 450 yards in length and 150 feet high, with its 15 generator turbines, would no longer supply the war production plants through the industrial section from Frankfurt to Hanover; nor could its gates be opened to flood the valley of the Eder River and hold up the American advance.

On March 31st, the division turned north and met the German 166th Infantry Division, just dispatched from Denmark. They were fresh to battle and put up a good defense against the 7th Armored. They were defending an east-west line through Kirchain, with most of their combat strength in the town. They put up a hard battle but were thoroughly beaten by the men and tanks of Combat Command R with support from CCB. For all practical purposes, the 166th was toast.

At this time Jack had an opportunity to catch up on his mail and read a letter from Jean that shocked him with its hostility. In a letter written by Jack before his son's birth on Christmas, Jean was upset that Jack had ideas of names other than Peter. Jack commented on having many more children in the same letter: "How about a dozen children?" She questioned, "Who I had been wearing myself out on?" His note back was straightforward.

> 31 March 1945 Germany
> Dear Jeannie and all,
>
> I received all my mail that had accumulated since I left for school, and I was quite happy to find so much of it.
>
> I was heartbroken to hear you have been so tired of late. I know how you must feel, as once in a while, we, too, lose a little sleep. I hope you are feeling better by the time you receive this letter.
>
> One note I received today indicated that you were upset about my suggestions for naming the child something other than Peter.

Also, over a remark I intended to be amusing. "How about a dozen children?" You seem to take offense and made quite a remark about "who I had been wearing myself out on." Well, old darling, afraid I must disappoint you, there has been only one gal I've been wearing myself out on, which is "Americana III," my tank. Let's do away with all that type of talk, etc. It is good only for causing ill feelings at its best, and my strongest desire is to have you trust me and continue that love that I knew so well before I left.

I realize that caring for our son is not easy, and I love you for being such a wonderful mother and perfect wife.

I imagine you have a pretty fair idea about where we are and what we are doing, and I would like to tell you more about it.

This evening, we were talking to a liberated Pole, who has been a slave laborer for over three years, and he said he was paid 25 marks a month ($2.50). One of the boys asked him what he did with all his money, and he got quite a kick out of them. He answered that "he played cards with it."

Well, my darling, I am quite tired this evening and must be up at 4:15, so I will hit the hay. Don't worry, I'm fine and will see you soon.

All my love

Jack

Jack quickly dashed a note to his parents that night, and told about being back with his team. He wrote that, "All of my boys were OK. They seemed glad to see me return from school, and I felt the same way to be with them again. They are a great bunch of men. One becomes rather attached to them after some of what we've been through together.

"One of the Polish laborers we liberated played his violin for us tonight. It was lovely. You cannot imagine how happy the Poles, Russians, French, Belgians, Dutch, and American prisoners whom we have liberated feel. They cry with joy after many have been slaves of the Germans for from 3 to 5 years."

CHAPTER SIXTEEN

The Heart of the Reich

The Ruhr Industrial Valley

The Ruhr had always been the beating heart of the Third Reich. It was Nazi Germany's main center of heavy industry, with coke plants, steelworks, armaments factories, and synthetic oil plants. The British had attempted to bomb it since 1940; however, at first it was to no effect because of the superiority of the Luftwaffe, massive air defense, and the lack of sophistication of British bombers.

As the RAF improved, it resumed bombing the Ruhr Valley in a five-month strategic campaign from March through July 1943. This was called the "Battle of the Ruhr." Targets included the Krupp armaments works in Essen, the Nordstern synthetic oil plant in Gelsenkirchen, and the Rheinmetal-Borsig plant in Dusseldorf. The British caused long delays for new armaments, damaged aircraft production for the Luftwaffe, and stopped the production of locomotives. Supplies of steel parts became unavailable for other manufactured products in Germany.

The Germans had other important industrial sectors farther east, which by the spring of 1945 had been overrun by the Red Army, leaving the Ruhr alone for Hitler to count on.

With the crossing of the Rhine River, the Western Front dynamically changed. Most German generals knew the war was effectively over and were more interested in saving soldier and civilian lives than saving the Reich. This became the common belief among the troops on both sides looking forward to the end of the war and going home.

To finish the war, Eisenhower knew that the Third Reich's most important heavy industrial heart still had to be conquered. Plans had been developed before the Normandy invasion, recognizing that it would be a hard-fought battle that could fail if the attack was head-on. Instead the plan was to encircle the Ruhr Valley with a classic pincer maneuver, with one army moving east on the north and one on the southern flank, then both armies meeting to close what became known as the Ruhr Pocket. The capture of the bridge at Remagen and the establishment of a bridgehead on the east side of the Rhine River was a lucky break that accelerated the Allied timetable.

General Hodges' First Army reconned the German 15th Army, which defended the southern portion of the Ruhr Valley east of the Rhine. Ike used this information to move the First Army east below the valley. He then had General Walter Simpson's Ninth Army advance east on the valley's north side.

There were a number of risks to the plan, but Eisenhower decided they were worth taking. For security reasons, the Ninth and First armies could not communicate with each other. Surprise was the key to success, with speed being the key element.

The reason for no communications was that the Germans and Allies used high-frequency intercept equipment known as Radio Direction Finder (RDF). Two or three RDF stations could isolate the exact position of a radio signal and attack it.

Hodges engaged the German Fifteenth Army's LXVII Corps, holding the southern flank of the Ruhr Valley. That corps had been engaged west of the Rhine with the First Army before the Allies crossed the river, and those engagements had severely weakened its strength. Once east of the Rhine, the German forces could not move or react quickly because of a shortage of supplies and fuel. Constant Allied air attacks interdicted supplies from reaching the Fifteenth Army by both road and rail.

Allied intelligence knew the supply status and layout of the German forces and used that knowledge to advance the First Army. The Germans were shocked by the speed of Hodges' forces which moved east twenty miles per day, devastating any Nazi resistance. Ninety miles were covered in five days.

Farther north, General William Simpson's US Ninth Army was attached to the British 21st Army Group under Field Marshal Montgomery. The Ninth was delayed in crossing the Rhine River to Wesel on the east side because of Montgomery's slowness in crossing the Rhine. After crossing the river, it was reassigned to the US 12th Army Group under the command of General Omar Bradley, as was the First Army.

The terrain east of Wesel was heavily wooded and marshy, slowing progress. Reconnaissance discovered that the German 116th Panzer Division was waiting ahead. Part of Montgomery's crossing plans included an airborne assault that stymied the 116th, allowing the Ninth Army, supported by its two armor divisions, to move slowly east while engaging Germans and the difficult terrain. With heavy artillery and tactical air support, Simpson broke through after a week.

Easter Sunday

> *Dawn and resurrection are synonymous. The reappearance of the light is the same as the survival of the soul.* — Victor Hugo

Easter Sunday has always been celebrated as a day of hope and prayer.

Jack attended an Easter service with the chaplain and was thinking about the challenges he would face going forward into the Ruhr Valley. He prayed for the safety of the men under his command and an end to the war so they could all return home to their families.

Unknown to Jack, Easter Sunday services were also being held for prisoners in nearby POW camps by Protestant and Catholic chaplains who were also prisoners. The guards stood by as the services took place, with large groups attending in open fields within the prison walls.

As John Toland wrote in *The Last 100 Days*: A group of American prisoners from the Battle of the Bulge were being marched from the POW camp Stalag 13 at Hammelburg (40 miles east of Frankfurt) to Bavaria. They had made it a third of the way and stopped near Nuremberg. Father Cavanaugh, a POW, came upon a small village Catholic Church. He talked with the local priest and borrowed his vestments to hold High Mass at 11:00. He had not entered a Catholic Church since he was captured in the Bulge. He addressed the 80 men in the church:

> This is the day that the Lord hath made; let us rejoice it…During the past four days, we have suffered our way of the cross, and we have suffered with the Christ who was represented in the wayside crucifixes that flanked our line of march.
>
> We have many blessings to ask Our Lord for. We ask him to continue His protection of us, to keep us free from sin, to help us be better men.

Tears ran down many cheeks, and Father Cavanaugh's own eyes were wet. "Easter is the feast of peace: peace between God and men, peace between nations, peace in political life, peace in home life, and peace in every child of God. Let us offer this Mass and Holy Communion so that peace may quickly come to this world."

The Pocket Is Closed that Afternoon

At the east end of the Ruhr Valley, the Ninth Army and the First Army met at the town of Lippstadt. Eisenhower's pincer maneuver had worked. The Ruhr was encircled into a 30 by 75-mile egg-shaped pocket. This was a staggering blow to German industrial might and efforts to continue the war.

Over 300,000 German troops were trapped inside the pocket. Field Marshal Walther Model's Army Group B was the parent command, with the 15th Army and the 5th Panzer Army. There were no fewer than 26 generals in the pocket and an admiral.

Model was the senior officer in the pocket and had enjoyed Hitler's praise for his skill and loyalty, gaining the nickname "The Führer's Fireman." As a defensive specialist, he excelled when put in the most dire situations. There was no question that he would fight to the death.

The Allies enjoyed air superiority, making it difficult for Model's commands to be resupplied from outside the Ruhr. Fuel was drastically needed, and food was in short supply for the troops and the 3.4 million civilians trapped in the area. Model requested that supplies be airlifted, but Germany no longer had such an ability.

Model believed that withdrawing his armies to central Germany would better defend the Reich. Hitler denied the request, believing that "Fortress Ruhr" would stall the hundreds of thousands of Allied troops for months.

In the end, Model felt the only solution was to fight out of the Ruhr Pocket through the Winterberg/Medebach area, where he felt the Americans were weakest. That plan was dropped as General Hodges's First Army moved its III Corps into that southern section.

Eighteen Divisions to the Ruhr Pocket

As the Ruhr Pocket was surrounded, most Allied troops continued the battle against the enemy, with General Patton's Third Army in the south moving toward Berlin and Field Marshal Montgomery's 21st Army Group in the north moving toward the Elbe River to eventually meet up with the Russians.

Eighteen US Divisions were consolidated around the Ruhr Pocket. Their mission was to liquidate the trapped German enemy. The first five days were used to get all the units of the various divisions in place for the final thrust planned for April 6th.

CHAPTER SEVENTEEN

7th Armored at the Rim of the Ruhr

The US First Army's III Corps included the 7th Armored Division, the 9th Infantry Division, which would later be replaced by the 5th Infantry Division, and the 99th Infantry Division.

The III Corps was to enter the Pocket on April 1st, advance northwestward from its current position, and clear all territory south of the Ruhr and east of the Lenne River. The 7th Armored would be in the center of the corps attack, with the 9th Infantry to its right and the 99th Infantry to its left. Their designated area had an estimated 100,000 Wehrmacht troops.

III Corps assigned the 7th Armored, jointly with the 9th Infantry Division, to lead the way in the advance. In turn, General Hasbrouck selected 7th Armored's Combat Command A, commanded by Colonel Andrew Adams, as the first element of the division to go into action.

Jack was part of CCA with his Company A of the 17th Tank Battalion. This was to be his first direct combat since being wounded and hospitalized in the last days of the Battle of the Bulge when St. Vith was recaptured from the Germans.

The 7th Armored was about to enter incredibly difficult countryside in which to fight a war. The Sauerland district is south of the Ruhr River, which flows west to the Rhine and west of the Lenne River, flowing north to the Ruhr. It is very mountainous, with heights between 900 and 1,500 feet. The transportation system has few wide roads. Most roads were narrow, or simply trails going through valleys between the mountains. Tanks and large military equipment had to travel single file and could easily be attacked from the cliffs and hills above the valley roads. Small rivers and mountain streams ran over 80% of the land, which was largely covered with forests.

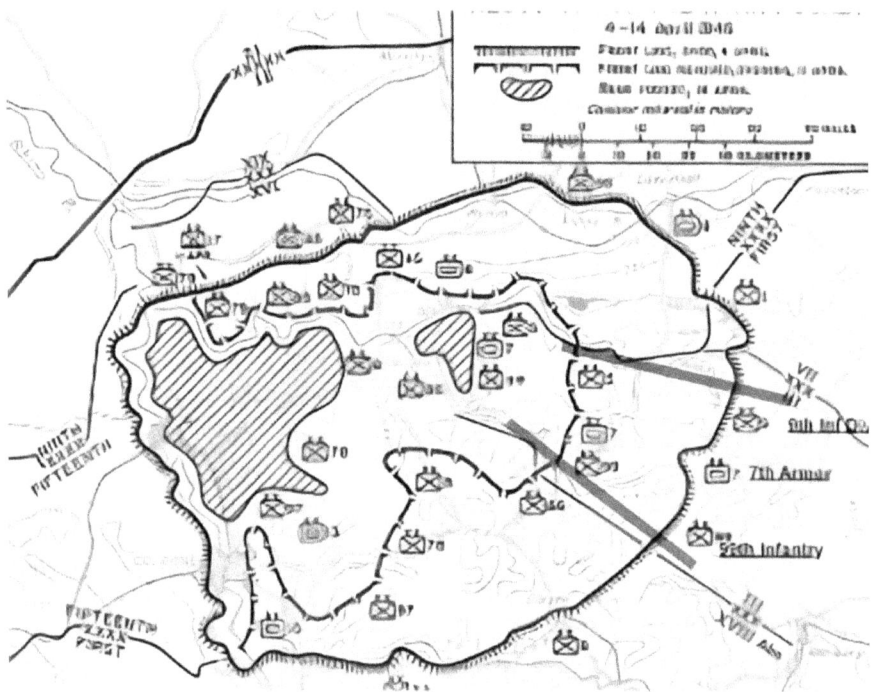

The German soldiers and Nazi SS had been protecting this area since 1939 and used their knowledge of the terrain to their advantage against the American forces.

First Army intelligence reported from various sources, including recently captured POWs, that the Germans would attempt to break out of the Ruhr Pocket at Medebach, so the 7th Armored's CCA was ordered to move to that town immediately to work with the 415th Infantry Battalion of the 9th Infantry Division and secure the area.

CCA moved out around 7:30 p.m. on April 2nd. A reconnaissance group took the lead. Task Force Wemple followed. Progress was very slow due to terrain, blackout conditions, and heavy rain. The roads forced the convoy to move single file. Vision to the front was so difficult that each tank had a GI ride on its front to let the driver know how close he was to the vehicle he was following.

Nearing Medebach, Lt. Colonel Wemple and his Intelligence Officer joined Colonel Adams to meet with the 415th Infantry to discuss the mission. CCA was to relieve the 415th in Medebach, where TF Wemple would be responsible for the town's defense and areas to the north and east.

When the task force arrived in Medebach, the 415th Infantry informed Col. Wemple that the Jerries, with about 150 panzergrenadiers and four tanks, had struck Medebach before dawn on April 1st. In the first flush of the attack, they gained a toehold in the western fringes of the town, but the 415th Infantry held fast, repelling them. The Americans captured a number of them and cleaned the high ground and woods to the north and northwest. Antitank guns knocked out one German tank; a bazooka accounted for another. The other two and those panzergrenadiers not killed or captured hastily retreated.

As German artillery constantly fell on the town, Wemple called his company commanders and platoon leaders forward to Medebach. They reconnoitered the area, and defensive positions and security were set up in and around the town.

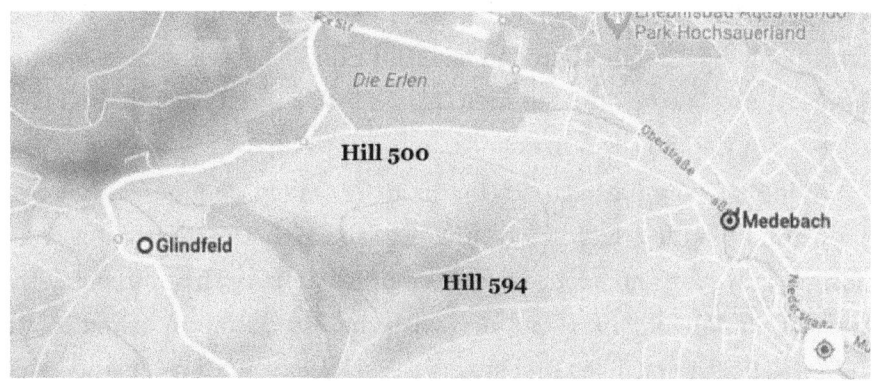

Task Force Wemple takes Glindfeld

With a few hours of rest after securing Medebach at 2:45 a.m., CCA, with the 415th Infantry Battalion, was ready to attack Glindfeld, a few miles due west behind a substantial height numbered Hill 500 (named for its height in meters). Plans were set to secure the hill to establish a fire base before proceeding to Glindfeld. Drawing some small arms fire from Hill 500, they reconned the surrounding terrain. There was an exposed half a mile of slightly rising ground to the heavily wooded hill that could handle tanks. The weather was favorable, with a morning haze that would soon clear for good vision.

Colonel Wemple called Jack over to where he was talking with Captain Dudley Britton. Dudley and Jack had paired up together when they were fighting to take back St. Vith in the final days of the Battle of the Bulge. Wemple asked Jack to help lead the charge to take Hill 500. Captain Dudley Britton was in the 23rd Armored Infantry Battalion.

Artillery was used to soften resistance on the hill as four platoons of tanks abreast, with GIs mounted on the tanks, moved toward the hill. The lefthand platoons veered to the left, but that side had jagged cliffs and was not passable. The two platoons fell back behind the other platoons in reserve – the righthand platoons, led by Jack and S/Sgt. Crutcher, flanked the hill. The GIs dismounted and proceeded through the woods, where eight enemy riflemen surrendered.

Jack took direct fire from Glindfeld and directed tank fire back at the town. They then proceeded under fire, with the infantry and tanks advancing together, to fight and take Glindfeld, capturing one German officer and 27 more enlisted men, transferring them back to the POW cage. They had no casualties.

While TF Wemple secured Glindfeld, TF Dailey, commanded by Major Thomas Dailey, Executive Officer of the 17th Tank Battalion, was assigned to take and secure the town of Kustelberg, five miles northwest of Medebach and Glindfeld, with the 3rd Battalion of the 145th Infantry Regiment. They met strong resistance from German anti-tank guns, tanks, and SP howitzers, keeping them at bay. At the same time, the infantry moved forward and reconned the locations of the enemy positions, sending target information back to the tanks, which were able to take out the German guns. After dark, they entered and secured the town.

One of the weapons the Germans used was a Hummel SP (self-propelled) gun. It had been a very successful weapon in the past two years against the Russians, and had also appeared in Normandy. It mounted a huge 150mm howitzer on a modified tank base, giving it both mobility and firepower.

CCA had a third task force, Task Force Rhea, commanded by Lt. Colonel Robert Rhea, Battalion Commander of the 23rd Armored Infantry.

With Kustelberg secured by TF Dailey, actions on April 4th began early. Jack told about their movement to Kustelberg from Medebach:

> We hit the road, which was wider than most of the roads we had traveled. The weather was cold, with light rain that turned into snow, as

we climbed the 5-mile trek to Kustelberg, rising 1,200 feet in altitude. The hills climbing to our right side had mostly evergreen trees with cliffs, perfect for Germans to hide and attack us from. All of us tankers rode with hatches up for visibility. The Nazis were well-trained and knew the territory like the back of their hand. We took on a lot of fire from long-range assault guns, artillery, and localized small-arms fire. I have to admit hearing bullets that whizzed by your tank and 88mm shells hit beside the road is scary. It gets many emotions in gear, but the main thought is protecting your team by managing your fear and keeping attentive to the surrounding terrain for the enemy. Fortunately, we had no casualties.

Attack on Hill 693

Upon arriving at Kustelberg, CCA ordered TF Wemple due west to secure Hill 693 and then the town of Gronebach, two miles beyond. TF Rhea was to pass through Kustelberg and take out the Germans occupying Hildfeld about 2.5 miles to the northwest. Task Force Dailey was to remain in Kustelberg, prepared to assist either task force.

When TF Wemple reached the western section of Kustelberg, the Germans were laying down heavy artillery and mortar fire; according to the maps, it was coming from Hildfeld to the northwest and Gronebach to the west. Seven GIs were injured by the enemy fire. The platoon leaders moved on foot to recon the terrain to Hill 693.

The weather was still overcast, with mild rain and intermittent snow. The terrain was soft farmland, and the tanks could handle moving to the hill, line abreast. They mounted up in their 11 Sherman tanks. Col. Wemple had them attack Hill 693 with Jack's tank platoon of four tanks abreast to the left of the hill. Another platoon went to the right, and the third platoon with three tanks stayed in reserve.

Jack's Sherman, dubbed *Americana III*, led the attack abreast with Sgt. Crutcher and two infantry platoons. They were met by heavy Jerry infantry resistance from small-arms fire, which pinned down the GIs.

There was much chaos as they fought their way through the woods. Jack's tanks were drawing both mortar and SP fire. One of the SP guns was taken out as they cleared the woods.

To the right, a panzer tank came into view and got a shot off, hitting Sgt. Crutcher's turret, "Blowing him to bits." Jack's tank crew had sights on the panzer and put a high-explosive round in its turret.

S/Sgt. Bill Crutcher had fought alongside Jack since his first combat experience on Thanksgiving Day. They went through the Battle of the Bulge together, and Sgt. Crutcher was an integral part of the "A" Company team. He was posthumously awarded the Silver Star for his heroism displayed that day.

Jack wrote in his notes in 1995 about the "firefight with a German panzer where my superior Platoon Sergeant Bill Crutcher was blown to bits in his tank next to me. He was from Missouri. The war was not far from being over, and to this day I mourn his death."

As the other tanks reached the open area, enemy SP gunfire from the north knocked out two more tanks. The remaining tank in the platoon finally knocked out the SP gun.

CCA decided to reorganize Task Force Wemple for the attack on Gronebach, and one platoon each of tanks and infantry were detached from TF Dailey and attached to TF Wemple.

During the reorganization, two platoons of GIs mounted on the tanks were assembled on the reverse slope of Hill 693, with the other platoon of tanks put in position to go around the north nose of the hill and attack along the east-west road. The two platoons assembled further south were to go over the crest of the hill and hit the town from the southwest. CCA's assault guns and mortars were in position and prepared to lay smoke in the woods to the south and west of the town. The artillery was prepared to shell the town on call. The enemy continued to spread mortar fire and artillery in the area during the re-organization.

Jack Given Command of Company C

Task Force Rhea had been attacking the town of Hildfeld, but the Germans fought hard, using every type of firepower they had available. During this attack, a platoon leader from Company C of the 17th Tank Battalion was killed, and the company commander, Lieutenant Cagle, was seriously wounded. TF Rhea captured and cleared the town around noon.

With Lt. Cagle being evacuated by the medics, Lt. Colonel Wemple moved Jack from Company A to take command of Company C in Task Force Rhea.

At 3:45, TF Rhea received orders from Combat Command A to assist Wemple in capturing the town of Gronebach. Jack took control of Company C and laid out the plan of attack, leading them in their movement from Hildfeld south to Gronebach. Along the way, they were shelled by SP howitzers and took a lot of sniper fire.

Company C attacked Gronebach at 4:15 with an infantry platoon mounted on a platoon of tanks and captured half of the town before Wemple's force entered from the south and east to capture the other half. The assault forces encountered small arms fire upon entering, but the force holding the town gave up rather quickly. TF Wemple took 43 POWs in the town.

After the clearing of Gronebach, Jack's team, both infantry and tanks, returned to Hildfeld to help consolidate and secure the town. They received intermittent artillery fire throughout the night.

A few days later, Jack shared the day with his parents. "I am now the commanding officer of our "C" company. The Company Commander was wounded, and I took over the other day in the middle of the fight and didn't know a man. What a deal that was."

Lt. Col. Wemple later wrote of Jack's actions in taking over C Company in a Battlefield Promotion Request in early May.

> When "C" Company Command was seriously wounded on 4 April 1945, Lieutenant Wilson was given command of that company. It was

in the midst of battle, and he did a terrific job leading the company through the remainder of the mission thrust upon his shoulders.

With assurance and outstanding aggressiveness, he mustered his company together, explained his desires, formulated the necessary plans for the operation, and led them forward in the battle.

With gallant abandon, he displayed courage far beyond his station and, on numerous occasions, was the subject of severe enemy sniper and artillery fire.

Although new to the company, he soon proved himself, and the men followed him with confidence and willingness.

Task Force Dailey had been dispatched earlier to take Niedersfeld, three and a half miles northeast of Gronebach. At 8:20 p.m., TF Wemple was ordered to proceed north to Niedersfeld and contact TF Dailey in Niedersfeld. They were to block all entrances to the town from the south and west and await further orders there. Consequently, the Task Force moved out immediately. They were delayed twice by roadblocks caused by fallen trees, but no enemy fire. In both cases, the engineer platoon cleared the road.

With security and roadblocks in place, they settled in for the night.

CHAPTER EIGHTEEN

The 7th Moves through Germany

Large numbers of Nazi anti-aircraft weapons, known as Flak guns (for Flugabwehrkanone), had been placed in the mountainous region of the Ruhr to protect the industry against Allied air attacks, and their crews and support units accounted for a considerable proportion of the German troops in the area.

Numerous small towns and villages comprised the center of the Ruhr industrial area, which shortened the enemy's lines of communication and gave the Nazi defenders the advantage of local supply. There seemed to be ample ammunition. With the advancement of the 7th Armored's Combat Command task forces, the Flak guns were converted to ground artillery and constantly rained down shells on the advancing forces.

Orders were delivered to the Task Force Commanders of CCA that first thing on the morning of April 5th, the three task forces were to move out and attack northwest from Niedersfeld into the Ruhr Pocket. The Germans had other plans, however; they flooded the valley with smoke, causing a delay in all the III Corps units.

Once the smoke cleared, Jack's Company C, spearheading the TF Rhea column, moved out to capture Wiemeringhausen, the first of many towns along the road to Wulmeringhausen. Fire from SP guns and artillery from a distance slowed the task force's progress. The Americans were fighting on a "one-tank front," battering slowly through narrow defiles as the Germans skillfully defended everything – roads, ridges, towns, and stream lines, using the terrain to their advantage.

At one point they reconned a German roadblock around a corner a quarter mile ahead. Jack ordered a first platoon tank with GIs aboard to move forward to take a defensive position, and then sent the doughs on foot to close in on the Nazis. Small arms and machine-gun fire came from the roadblock. The infantry, after a short firefight, cleared the roadblock, killing four and taking eight prisoners. The engineers used a tank dozer to clear the roadblock.

Jack continued towards Wiemeringhausen. As Task Force Rhea was about to enter the town, they encountered a large roadblock supported by anti-tank and SP guns, mortars, and 20mm Flak guns along with small arms. The area was flat, so for once it was easy for Jack's Shermans to maneuver. Jack sent a platoon of tanks with GIs riding to the right side of the roadblock and another to the left. The tankers zeroed in on the anti-tank and SP guns with their 75mm cannons and took out the larger guns, and the GIs advanced on foot to engage the Germans at the roadblock. After a 15-minute firefight, the obstacle was cleared.

The Task Force continued into the town, where there was mild resistance. About 45 Germans surrendered, and the town was cleared and secured around 1:00 in the afternoon.

They continued north to Assinghausen, where they encountered two roadblocks along the two miles. They were easily cleared. Once in the town, the resistance was light. Jack encountered and surrounded a small group of Waffen SS. He was surprised that despite their reputation they put up so little resistance. He confronted the SS officer and told him to surrender: "He pulled his sidearm, and I killed him. We then moved the rest of the captured troops to the POW cages."

With Assinghausen cleared and secured, the American column moved north. Lt. Colonel Rhea told Jack to take half the task force to seize Bruchhausen while he took Wulmeringhausen.

CCA attached an infantry company from the 47th Infantry Regiment to support the attack on Bruchhausen. They met stubborn resistance, and the terrain would not allow a direct path for the tanks to attack. He had the armor units move west, circle north, and back east to the main north/south road into Bruchhausen.

With the task force in position, the tanks moved out on the assault, south on the main road. As soon as they reached the crest of a hill, they drew heavy anti-tank fire from the town. The enemy took out one of the Shermans on the right flank. Jack had the other tanks pull back in a defilade-protected area. Forward observers were deployed near the crest of the hill and communicated gun positions in the town. As German artillery continued to rain on their position, the tanks returned fire with 75mm high-explosive shells at the Jerry positions.

With the support of the 47th, the infantry was put in a position to assault. Artillery and tank cannons were used to pin down the Germans before the task force entered the town.

There was a long and hard-fought firefight between the tank-supported GIs and German panzers throughout the town, devastating buildings and homes. Jack grimly reported:

> After the fighting subsided, I directed a block-by-block search to ensure all enemy troops were captured. Sergeant Oliver, one of my platoon leaders, called me to one home. One of the doughboys reported that women and children were screaming in the home's cellar. I had the doughs check it out to see if they could get them out. Unfortunately, they were trapped and were going to burn to death. I ordered a tank to fire a high explosive shell into the cellar; it was the worst experience I can remember.

Jack had shared very little about his war experiences with the family, this being one of the few times. As he told it to his children and shared it with his grandchildren, he would talk about not having the benefit of time as he could hear the screams coming from the burning house and had to decide whether to let them die slowly as they burned to death or end it quickly with the high-explosive shell. He was very emotional as he told the story, and those listening felt the pain that he lived with over this horrendous event. He said, "War was hell on earth and sometimes worse. I pray that none of you experience it."

After securing Bruchhausen, his task force left and rejoined the rest of Task Force Rhea in Wulmeringhausen later that evening. Meeting with Lt. Colonel Rhea, Jack briefed him on the actions and results in Bruchhausen. Rhea briefed Jack on his own progress that day, and the task force settled in for the night.

CCA summarized the day in its After-Action Report:

> It had been a long, tough day as the three task forces took Wiemeringhausen, Assinghausen, Bruchhausen, Olsberg, Bigge – and many other villages that are hard to find on a map. All the villages were occupied and defended by German troops that erupted in firefights, generally ended quickly by the task forces. POWs were sent to the local POW cage for processing.

April 6th: The Final Assault Begins

Task Force Dailey was to pass through Olsberg and Bigge – both towns in friendly hands – on the morning of April 6th, on its way to capture Antfeld, three miles to the northeast.

Task Force Rhea, with Jack's Company C leading, was to follow TF Dailey and turn southwest at Bigge to capture the town of Helmeringhausen.

The morning started normally with some incoming artillery and small arms fire. The task force stopped in Olsberg for fuel and ammunition. Jack was with his platoons of Company C, getting the tanks fueled up next to his old Company A, which was doing the same, fetching ammo for their tank cannon. He had just had a chat with his old driver, Tech. Sergeant Dudley, and Corporal Louie Brodman, his old gunner on Americana III.

As TF Rhea was mounting up to leave Olsberg, its units came under sniper fire, and Cpl. Brodman was hit in the head and killed about 50 feet from where Jack was standing. It was devastating for Jack and his old company.

Jack shared his thoughts in a letter to his father:

> My old gunner from my tank, America's III, was killed by a sniper a short distance from where I was with my new company. It knocked the old gang to pieces, especially as a few days before, we had a little scrape, my America's III tank, and all of my platoon came out of it. We were lucky. I lost some other fine fellows that day. It's a pretty rugged life at times.
>
> My old driver, Dudley, was evacuated for combat fatigue after Louie was killed. We had shared various tanks since I joined 7th Armor.
>
> I wish it were over. All the boys in the old outfit are pretty broken up about Louie. They said that if a soldier went to heaven, Louie was there.

Why do people have to kill and fight? It seems pretty stupid to me. We are making the bastards pay dearly, too. I have absolutely no use for either the soldiers or the civilians. Each is as dangerous as the other. Nazi artillery can shell us, and the German people will not believe that it is Jerry's stuff. Beats me.

Jack was thinking about Dudley. Remembering a conversation they'd had after his first combat experience when they discussed their experiences in California and how times had changed them, they wondered how different they would be when they got home.

Dudley had seen so much since arriving in Europe. Fighting in France, Belgium, Holland, the Battle of the Bulge, and here in the Ruhr Pocket, surviving death and losing so many friends, how much could one man handle?

Task Force Rhea takes Helmeringhausem

The task force moved out through Olsberg and Bigge, turning southwest for two miles to attack the town of Helmeringhausen. Along the way, they overcame three lightly defended roadblocks.

The assault began around 3:00 in the afternoon, with the GIs leading on foot and Jack's tanks following. The Germans put up small resistance and the town was secured and cleared around 5:00. Helmeringhausen was organized for defense around 9:00 p.m. and the task force remained in the town for the night. Sixteen POWs were sent to the cage.

On the morning of April 8th, the 23rd Armored Infantry Battalion, including Jack's C/17 of Task Force Rhea, was relieved of its defensive position at Helmeringhausen. It was moved to Winterberg, where the full 7th Armored Division was bivouacked. Jack's Company was released to the 17th Tank Battalion as all three task forces, Rhea, Wemple, and Dailey, were dissolved.

The 17th had been in battle every day since April 2nd. All the units needed this rest to maintain their vehicles, weapons, and equipment.

Jack could also finally take a little break and write to Jean and his parents. He told his parents, "Company 'C' is a good unit, and I am pleased with their combat action. We're getting a slight pause for station identification and a little rest for a few days. The men need it, as they have been going very hard since crossing the Rhine River."

During this respite, Task Force Rhea was reconstituted and deployed west as part of Combat Command B while the rest of the 17th Battalion was held in temporary reserve.

Task Force Rhea was reassigned three days later to Combat Command A. They were in Isingheim after spending the last few days attacking and clearing a number of small towns. They were ordered to Eslohe, about four miles away, and regrouped with Company C. Jack took the company from Winterberg 30 miles through 7th Armored Division-controlled roads, meeting up with Lt. Colonel Rhea at 4:00 in the afternoon.

The 7th Armored would attack with two combat commands abreast, CCA on the north, or right side, and CCR on the southern left side. CCB would be in reserve. CCA was given a specific route of attack, and it was to be made with task forces in column. TF Rhea would lead with one company of the 395th Infantry Regiment attached, followed by the 489th Field Artillery Battalion, TF Wemple, and TF Dailey.

The task forces attacked targets along the route, leapfrogging each other; once the target was cleared, each task force went forward to attack the next target. The GIs rode on the tanks. To shorten the column as much as possible, only essential vehicles for the mission were taken.

These movements of the 7th Armored Division marked the first day on which the armored units could move out ahead of infantry formations, speeding the attack against the entrenched German forces.

Task Force Rhea included the 23rd Armored Infantry Battalion, 395th Infantry Regiment, and Jack's Company C. GIs without halftracks rode on the tanks as they attacked towns and villages in the center of the mountainous area southeast of Essen and Dusseldorf.

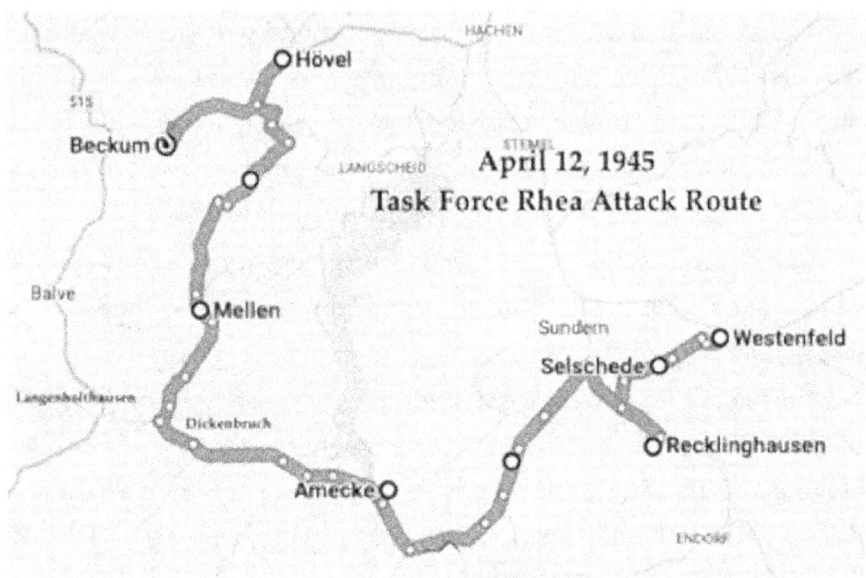

The task force moved to rendezvous with the other units of CCA in the area of Westenfeld. Thereafter, TF Rhea's first target was to capture Selschede. They met moderate resistance from the Nazis and cleared the town quickly to move southeast to capture Recklinghausen, which was cleared of the enemy around 11:00.

Many of these villages had small manufacturing facilities supporting the industry in larger cities like Essen. From a military standpoint, they were primarily hubs of anti-aircraft units protecting the Ruhr industrial valley. The Americans next attacked the town of Siedfeld. There was modest resistance from SP howitzers and the always-present Flak anti-aircraft guns. Jack's tankers took out the SP guns, and the GIs silenced the Flak guns, clearing the town of the enemy around noon. TF Dailey and TF Wemple were clearing other villages to the left and right of TF Rhea.

Task Force Rhea continued the attack to the southwest towards Amecke, where moderate resistance was encountered in small villages en route. As Lt. Colonel Wemple discussed in the 17th Tank Battalion After-Action Report: "Until this time, TF Rhea had made excellent progress at the head of the combat command column and had met with very little enemy resistance, although they had taken prisoners at almost every town."

When TF Wemple reached Siedfeld, they found that TF Rhea had met rather stubborn resistance at Amecke, and that there were still some determined enemy troops in that area that had not been destroyed or captured.

Lt. Colonel Rhea had Jack dispatch tank platoons with GIs onboard to clear out the local activity, which was accomplished in short order. Then the effort was concentrated on Amecke, clearing the town by 1:30 in the afternoon. The captured Germans were sent to the POW cage, and all enemy equipment was destroyed. They continued to two small villages that no longer exist on a German map, Bruchhausen and Kasberg, clearing the small opposition and moving to Dickenbruch,

Colonel Adams, commander of Combat Command A, called for a meeting with his three task force commanders in Dickenbruch, just southeast of Langenholthausen. Instructions were given for TF Rhea to go north to capture Mellen. TF Wemple was to take Langenholthausen, just to the west, and proceed north to Balve. TF Dailey was to back up Wemple.

CCA deployed the 489th Armored Field Artillery Battalion north of Dickenbruch in a position that could support all three task forces and provide constant artillery support.

TF Rhea's infantry companies moved out on foot for the 1.5-mile march to Mellen while the tanks and other support vehicles loaded ammunition and fueled up in Dickenbruch. They captured Mellen with little resistance, taking a large number of POWs and clearing the town by 4:30.

As they drove north, a few more villages appeared. Melschede showed little resistance and was cleared in 30 minutes. Continuing north they attacked Hovel, where enemy resistance was very light, and the town was easily cleared. The task force set up security defenses for the night in Hovel.

It had been a long day for Lt. Colonel Rhea's 23rd Armored infantry and Jack's tank company with constant fighting, dodging bullets, and getting the Germans to surrender. They succeeded with approximately 1,000 POWs taken by Task Force Rhea that day.

Meantime, Task Forces Wemple and Dailey had left Dickenbruch to attack the much larger town of Langenholthausen to the northwest. There the Nazi defenders put up a strong fight, though two hours later it was cleared and secured. They then succeeded in taking Balve and the two task forces hunkered down for the night. CCA established its command post in Langenholthausen at 9:00 p.m.

President Roosevelt Dies

President Roosevelt died that night in Warm Springs, Georgia. The American public grieved, but there was a different view in Nazi Germany.

As bombs were raining down on Berlin, Goebbels took great delight in telling Hitler over the phone that the stars had aligned and a miracle that would save the Third Reich – as in earlier days had saved Frederick the Great – had come to pass.

"Mein Führer!" Goebbels exclaimed. "I congratulate you! Roosevelt is dead."

In an order of the day two days later, Hitler proclaimed, "At the moment when fate has removed the greatest war criminal of all time from the earth, the turning point of this war shall be decided."... Toland, *The Last 100 Days*

The Division Sets Up for Final Closure

Task Force Rhea spent time in Hovel maintaining vehicles and equipment. At 10:45, they traveled southwest to capture Beckum. The German resistance was intense, as they came under heavy artillery fire from SP guns and several tanks. There were no casualties as they continued their attack.

GIs dismounted from two of Jack's tank platoons and led the charge into enemy machine guns and small arms fire as the tankers backed them up with machine-gun and cannon fire. The other platoons concentrated on the anti-tank, SP artillery, and panzers, taking the town down and clearing it around 3:00 p.m.

TF Wemple was en route north from Balve to Volkringhausen, where it had been stopped by a heavily fortified roadblock, which they attacked and cleared. As they continued north, another German roadblock was created by blowing overhead rail tracks and a bridge over a wide, swollen stream. CCA contacted TF Rhea for support to help clear this one.

A platoon of Jack's tanks with infantry and a tank dozer met Wemple at the rail underpass. TF Wemple's tank dozer, a retriever, and engineers were working on clearing the block. A recon was made for a bypass route, but it was determined that installing a small portable bridge and removing the roadblock could be done quicker than bypassing the obstacle.

Wemple deployed infantry across the stream to advance on Volkringhausen by foot while clearing the roadblock. The infantry troops fought a small German detachment and caused them to surrender before the rest of the task force cleared the roadblock and joined them. They then moved north and captured the town of Binolen. The town was cleared and secured for the night.

TF Dailey was scheduled to take Brockhausen. The I&R platoon (Intelligence and Reconnaissance) immediately made a reconnaissance of the routes to the west and found that it was impossible to get the task force across the terrain at that point. The woods were dense, and the terrain was so soft and muddy that it would bog down the tanks and other heavy equipment. CCA concurred, and TF Dailey moved north and then west to capture the town of Deilinghofen on the road leading to Hemer. The resistance was light, with most Germans surrendering.

TF Rhea consolidated its position in Beckum after the platoon completed its support mission. Approximately 75 POWs had been taken. Combat Command A set up its command post in Beckum to manage the capture and defeat of the Nazis in Hemer – the final mission in the Ruhr Pocket for the 7th Armored Division.

CHAPTER NINETEEN

Closing the Pocket

Combat Command A Positioned for Final Assault

By this time, the Ruhr Pocket was split into two parts, and knowledge of this was widespread among the Germans opposing the American advance. Very few of Germany's Wehrmacht were putting up a fight and the vast majority were surrendering en masse. CCA's mission was to surround Hemer for a final assault.

Model Asked to Surrender

Field Marshal Walther Model, the commanding general of German Army Group B, was met by an aide to General Matthew Ridgway of the XVIII Airborne Corps and was asked to surrender. Model refused.

Model's chief of staff asked him to contact Hitler for permission to surrender. Model knew what the Führer's answer would be, and knew as well that he could not personally surrender because of all the sacrifices he had asked of his officers and troops over the years. The news, both within and outside the Ruhr Pocket, was hopeless. Model struggled with a solution, believing every life saved could help rebuild Germany. He decided to dissolve Army Group B. There could not be a formal surrender of a command that no longer existed.

Model decreed on April 15th that all youths and older men would immediately be discharged from the army to go home. Two days later, it was estimated, all ammunition and supplies would be exhausted. All remaining non-combatants were free to surrender. Combatants could either fight in organized groups and attempt to escape the pocket or try to make their way in civilian clothes or uniforms without weapons to their homes. This constituted a veiled authority to surrender.

On the morning of April 14th, the 7th Armored Division made its final assault on Hemer with Combat Command A leading the central attack.

TF Wemple moved out of Binolen at 6:00 a.m. The terrain was hopelessly canalized with a stream and railroad grade on the left and high cliffs on the right. Colonel Wemple ordered the infantry to precede the tanks, two platoons abreast, one taking advantage of all possible cover and concealment on the left of the road and the other on the right to continue the attack to the north. The platoon on the left received only a few rounds of small arms fire and flushed out 16 Germans who surrendered.

While the I&R platoon had been scouting a route to Brockhausen, the column continued to advance toward the town of Hannethal, which intersected with the passable road leading west to Hemer. By 10:00, the task force was at the underpass at Hannethal, drawing several rounds of direct fire from Hemer.

TF Rhea relieved TF Wemple, taking over the position at Hannethal. Lt. Colonel Rhea deployed half the task force to attack the towns of

Riemke and Apricke, three miles east of Hemer. Jack was left in command of the remainder of the task force.

Small arms fire and Flak guns caused light delay before Riemke but was quickly silenced. The Germans in Apricke, supported by artillery and self-propelled gunfire, made a stronger resistance, which the infantry quelled. They continued to attack west of Apricke for a mile, clearing all the Germans in the woods. TF Rhea was to stay in place for the final assault on Hemer.

The I&R Platoon reported to Colonel Wemple that they had found a good route to reach the town of Brockhausen, so Wemple's column turned around and moved out for Brockhausen on the trail located by the recon. When they reached Baingsen, a little settlement about halfway between the highway and Brockhausen, they found that friendly infantry had reached Baingsen and taken over 200 POWs without a fight. They moved on into Brockhausen without firing a shot and found over 100 enemy soldiers ready to surrender.

As Wemple entered Brockhausen, Nazi artillery fire and 88mm air blasts came from several guns to the west. By noon, the task force had cleared Brockhausen. Defenses were set up and the town secured. Additional German troops were still coming in from the north and west of the town to surrender. TF Wemple had more than 200 POWs from all types of units, but most were anti-aircraft crews that were supposed to defend the airfield just east of the town of Hemer.

At 1:30, the Executive Officer of CCA ordered TF Rhea to be relieved at Hannethal. The task force moved north to an airfield east of Hemer and seized the high ground alongside TF Wemple. The attack was made with two platoons of tanks abreast, with GIs riding on the tanks and one platoon following the assault wave by about 400 yards.

As the attack was taking place, the force was receiving incoming fire from Nazi 105mm howitzers, and large air bursts with what was estimated to be 40mm and larger anti-aircraft guns. The fire was coming from the high ground to the east of Hemer. The AA guns on the airfield were not manned, and the Americans did not receive any fire from the woods, which was their objective; as soon as the tanks reached the woods, 50 more POWs were taken with no resistance.

Lt. Col. Wemple described the attack:

> This attack was the most picturesque we have ever participated in or observed. The terrain was excellent for the tanks, and they moved in at about 15 MPH.
>
> The formation was perfect, and the enemy artillery fire and air bursts were sufficient to make it more than a dry run; in fact, many of the rounds were very close misses, and, surprisingly, we suffered no casualties.
>
> We believe that even if the AA guns on the airfield had been manned, the objective would have been gained with minimal losses.

Jack was charged with deploying tanks and tank destroyers to fire into Hemer when the final assault was to take place. He also had a little time to write a letter to Jean and Peter:

> I have been swamped in the operational sense of the word and haven't had time to write a line for several days. I am writing this from a landing strip we liberated somewhere in Germany, and the artillery one has to duck around here is strictly scandalous.
>
> I got a letter from Ruth Ann Wilson. She and Mickey are now in the Ninth Army in an Evac. Hospital. She said the artillery gives her the jitters. Well, it might. It is good that they are not here, where one receives and deals it out.
>
> The Company is doing great. They are all real combat veterans, and we see eye-to-eye. I hope I can bring them all through the rest of the fight.

Task Force Danube of the 99th Infantry Division – the 3rd Battalion of the 395th Regiment – was temporarily attached to Combat Command A and moved out from Beckum at 8:00 a.m. to seize Sundwig, 1.5 miles south of Hemer. They met moderate artillery and anti-tank fire resistance, securing the town by 1:00 p.m. They were instructed to hold their position for the attack on Hemer.

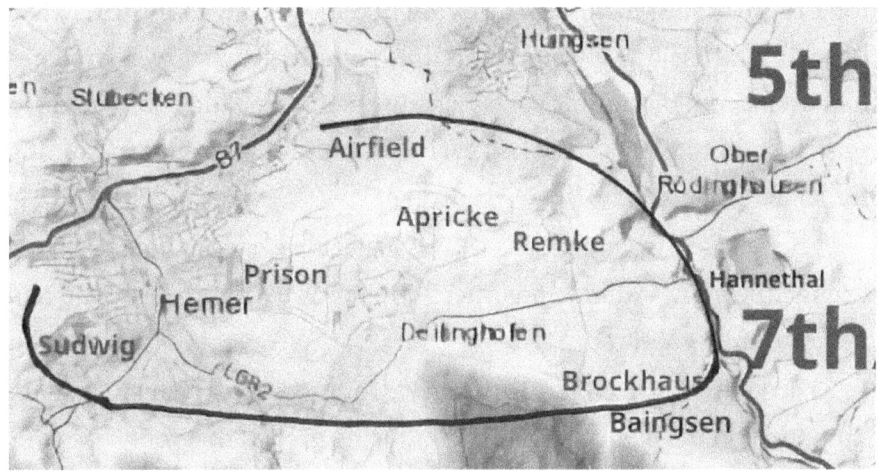

TF Dailey took the town of Deilinghofen with little resistance and headed toward the eastern end of Hemer, where they encountered a German officer with a white flag. The officer informed Major Dailey that he was approaching a German POW camp with 23,000 starving and dying prisoners. His concern was about the release of them if the town were attacked and the chaos that would ensue. Dailey instructed the German officer to keep control of the camp until some American forces could take over.

Major Dailey entered the town of Hemer and was escorted to a German headquarters to discuss the town's surrender. This negotiation continued until late in the afternoon when the 7th Armored Division refused the terms of the German commanding general. There was a cease-fire during the negotiations, which gave time to get the POW camp under control.

Hemer POW Camp

The Hemer POW camp was one of the largest to be liberated. The leading troops from the 17th Tank Battalion arrived and witnessed the horrible sight of humans squeezed into the limited area of the Nazi open-air stockade, digging in the ground with their bare hands, searching, groveling, and fighting for grubs and worms to eat. They had been alone without food for over a week and were dying like flies treated with DDT. The German guards had fled, and thousands of these poor, starved wretches had broken out of their prison stockade and flooded the countryside in search of food. They ransacked every place they came across, hunting for something to eat.

The 23,000 prisoners were 84% Russian. Other nationalities included French, Belgian, Italian, and others, including 99 Americans who had been recently captured.

Through interpreters using truck-mounted loudspeaker systems, they stopped the camp's exodus by assuring groups that food was coming. It did arrive in a matter of an hour. Many who broke away returned quickly when word spread that food was being distributed. This incident, however, required the services of an entire battalion of the 99th Infantry Division, which had to be withdrawn from their offensive at Iserlohn to maintain order in the vicinity of the camp.

In the POW hospital building, housing the sickest of the prisoners, the Germans had put three dying men in each bed. The German guards had lived in luxury in the same building, two guards to a room. How civilized humans could treat others in such outrageous fashion surpassed all understanding.

As the 99th took over and brought them food and medical attention, the German medical personnel who remained were dismayed when they were hurled out of their rooms so that fatally sick soldiers could be placed in them.

With the POW camp secured and attack plans in place, at 8:30 in the evening, Hemer was attacked. TF Danube of the 99th Infantry attacked and secured Hemer with TF Rhea, TF Wemple, and TF Dailey prepared to support with direct fire across their front if needed.

The 7th Armored Division had accomplished its mission in the Ruhr Valley. III Corps ordered the relief of the 7th, turning over the area to the 99th Infantry Division.

Order of the Day

In an Order of the Day dated 19 April 1945 from Major General Robert W. Hasbrouck to the officers and men of the 7th Armored Division, their part in the collapse of the Ruhr Pocket was outlined in the following extract:

> The 7th Armor mission was to chop up the pocket you helped to create. Despite the mountainous terrain greatly favoring the enemy, you drove to the heart of his defenses. That part of the Pocket you were to reduce ceased to exist at 8:45 on 16 April – good hunting.

Field Marshal Model Commits Suicide

During the last few days of the collapse, Field Marshal Model asked his chief of staff, "What is left for a commander in defeat?" He paused, then answered his own question. "In ancient times, they took poison."

Those who knew him intimately knew he would never surrender. Model had been critical of Field Marshal Friedrich Paulus for becoming a Russian prisoner at Stalingrad. "A Field Marshal can't do that. Such a thing is just not possible."

On the afternoon of April 21st, Model asked his aide to accompany him as he walked deeper into the forest, away from the rest of his staff. Then he committed suicide with his pistol.*

---

* Letter, Maj Hansgeorg Model to U.S. Army Historical Office, Europe, 29 Mar 66, filed in OCMH. Model's aide buried the field marshal, marked the grave, and after the war identified it for the field marshal's son, who later had the body reinterred in a soldier's cemetery in the Huertgen Forest, among the graves of men the field marshal had commanded.

CHAPTER TWENTY

To the Baltic

After the success of the last two weeks, the 7th Armored Division was relieved of its responsibilities at the Ruhr Pocket. It was time to move east to a new assembly area in Gottingen, Germany. Jack's C Company of the 17th Tank Battalion led Task Force Rhea as the lead unit of Combat Command A, which led the 7th Armored Division for the 160-mile movement. CCA received the warmest praise from the commanding general of the veteran 9th Infantry Division for its support in the Ruhr Pocket.

The 17th Tank Battalion moved south several miles to the town of Rosdorf, where it settled in and devoted itself to maintaining vehicles and weapons, completely unloading all vehicles, washing them, and restoring them. A command inspection was scheduled for the following morning.

Jack was delighted to catch up on the letters he had received from Jean, which had only been mailed ten days earlier in Spokane. Jean included one from their five-month-old son Peter, which was a fun surprise.

He responded that he enjoyed the letters, kept on top of his work, and could finally tackle his correspondence.

> We are in a little German town "rehabilitating." It is restful and far from the sound of artillery. I have good billets for my men, and most have beds to sleep in.

Jack's Story | **175**

Today, my company and vehicles were inspected by the battalion. When that was finished, I went to Rear Echelon, got the payroll, and paid off the men, which is quite a long job.

After I paid them, a couple of my boys came dashing in saying, "Lt., the general is outside and wants to see you." Gad! Rank doesn't bother me, Not much! I went outside, and there he was, both Silver Stars shining. He wanted to inspect my tanks, so I took him around the company, and the men were strictly on the ball, reporting, etc.... I was very proud of them, and he appeared quite satisfied with the tour.

I must seem like an old person to you when I say that I think the "C" Company is as good as the "A" Company and perhaps better in some respects. I am very happy here. I have a wonderful unit of men; they love to fight, and once more, they are veterans and know how to handle themselves. It is a thrill to see them operate in some of our attacks.

Jack told her about visiting Kassel a few days before with Chris Chrisman. They had both seen the destruction of Aachen and Cologne, which was devastating, but Kassel was much worse. "I was truly amazed."

Chris had been head of the supply train of the 7th Armored Division and knew Jack's wife from their time at Fort Knox. Jean described their home as the local frat house. Jack told her they saw each other almost daily while they were in reserve.

Jack seemed not to have a dull moment. On the march from Hemer to Gottingen, some of the tanks had been damaged due to speed, and Jack finished a paper on "March Discipline" for Colonel Triplet of Combat Command A. He then presented the paper to the officers' school and his company.

It was also time to get busy on the Information & Education program, as several men in the battalion were anxious to study some courses by correspondence. Just as in college, when he joined ROTC along with his studies and volunteered for every other public service in sight, Jack kept his finger in a variety of pies. There was also time, however, for recreation.

In a new letter to Jean a few days later, Jack told her the story about he and Chris finding an open cognac place. However, they were informed that there was only one restriction: they had to purchase more than one bottle. "Ah, Oui, we took many bottles." They were given to the men in their units, but some they saved for their own consumption. Jack laughed about wading through the cognac on the place's floor, about four inches deep. "I have never seen anything like it in my life."

All the men looked forward to the opportunity to bathe, so Jack joined Doc Wheeler and the Chaplain and traveled to the next town, where they could take a bath and get some clean uniforms.

As the "Occupation and Military Government" was getting established, there were strict rules against troops fraternizing with local civilians. Jack mentioned to Jean that this non-fraternization policy was quite difficult to control. He guessed that some men would do anything.

As the 7th Armored Division continued in reserve, Germany continued to splinter, and the days of Hitler's Third Reich were coming to an end.

Eisenhower Comes Face to Face with the Holocaust.

The 4th Armored Division and the 89th Infantry of the Third US Army liberated Ohrdruf, the first Nazi concentration camp liberated by American troops, on April 4, 1945.

On April 12th, Generals Dwight Eisenhower, Omar Bradley, and George Patton visited the Ohrdruf camp, part of the Buchenwald system. It was small compared to camps discovered later; nevertheless Eisenhower was unprepared for the Nazi's brutality. Ike refused to leave immediately and spent time meeting with former prisoners, visiting every building, and getting a full sense of this atrocious "Hell on Earth." He had already seen the brutality of the Nazi POW camps, but these didn't come close in savagery to the concentration camps.

Eisenhower realized that his men were fighting not only for territory but for ridding Europe of the barbarism of Hitler's Third Reich.

He realized that someday the Holocaust might be denied, so the media was invited in to record the horrors. He also made local citizens tour the facility and asked General George Marshall to have President Truman encourage members of the US Congress to visit the camps.

Based on his experience and the discovery of other concentration camps, like Bergen-Belsen, Ike issued a series of orders:

- All survivors were to be cared for and interviewed.
- All camps were to be documented, photographed, and filmed.
- German citizens near the camps were ordered to help bury the dead, care for the living, and witness what had been done in their name.
- All forces under his command were to visit liberated camps as they moved through the areas of the camps.

Bergen-Belsen

Bergen-Belsen had been established in 1940 as an Allied prisoner-of-war camp. In 1943, the SS took over and made it a Nazi concentration camp. As the Russians advanced through Eastern Europe, the SS marched Jewish prisoners west to Bergen. Ann Frank, the diarist, and her father were the most famous prisoners in the camp. They both died in March, only 30 days before the British arrived.

As the British were advancing towards the Belsen camp, a German envoy requested a local truce for the area surrounding the camp, explaining that diseases such as typhus were endemic. His fear was that open combat would allow inmates to escape and spread disease to German civilians and soldiers, and British troops.

British reconnaissance verified the camp's presence and the truce was agreed on April 12th, so no shots were fired. The German and Hungarian guards would remain to guard the camp until relieved by the British.

On April 15th, the Nazis continued strong resistance outside the neutral zone. The 63rd Anti-Tank Regiment of the Royal Artillery finally entered the camp. The British troops had witnessed horrendous death and destruction through the last five years of war, but to a man, no one was prepared for what they found.

There were over 60,000 starving prisoners in need of medical attention and sustenance. They found over 13,000 corpses unburied and rotting. The camp contained an array of not just Jews but others the Nazis found inferior or enemies of the state, representing 20 different nationalities. A Russian prisoner-of-war camp was also part of the complex in the same cruel existence.

The British immediately started a humanitarian effort to help the survivors.

The war would soon end, and most combat had ceased. Jack had just survived the deadly combat of the Ruhr Pocket and was moving to the Baltic area to stop any German troops coming back from Norway through Denmark to support the last gasps of the Third Reich.

On April 29th, the 7th Armored was reattached to Montgomery's 21st Army Group, moving to an Elbe River bridgehead and the approaches to the Baltic Sea. The division's first movement from Rosdorf was to Eschede, which was 20 miles from the Bergen-Belsen Concentration Camp.

On May 1st, 1945, tankers from the 7th Armored Division, as reported in the history of the 31st Tank Battalion, visited the camp. Jack was one of them.

Years later he shared a few war events with his family and children, including visiting Bergen-Belsen. It was when his family lived in Topeka, Kansas; Dr. Karl Menninger and his wife Jean were at the house for dinner. Dr. Karl was the Chief of Psychiatry for the Army during World War II and the head of the Menninger Foundation with his brother Will in Topeka.

The conversation turned to the war, and the subject of the Holocaust was raised. It was then that Jack Wilson related his visit to the Bergen-Belsen and relived his experience.

He excused himself from the table and returned with a large vanilla envelope, which he set on the table. "Here are the pictures I took the day I visited Bergen-Belsen." There was silence as he sorted some out to share with Dr. Karl. He went on to say that he had seen many horrors in combat and POW camps, which he was involved in liberating: "But nothing prepared me for what I experienced that day. I had no knowledge these death factories existed."

> The stench was overwhelming as we departed our vehicles and walked into the camp, even though the British had worked hard over the last few weeks. As you can see in the pictures, the former prisoners were skeletons of their former selves, having only received food since the British arrived and fed only a little at a time to let them come back to health. But they still looked like the Walking Dead. These people had been beaten and starved. They were tortured and denied anything that would make life livable.
>
> We were free to walk around the camp; there were large graves where the Nazis had tried to hide the dead, and thousands were being dug up by local Germans and moved for a proper burial. Other piles of dead people were stacked like wood. I was informed that the people were given no water and seldom served food. Often, no food was given on orders of the camp's commandant. There were 500 deaths a day from starvation even though there were sufficient rations available, but the orders were to let the prisoners die from hunger.
>
> It will be a day and experience embedded in me for the rest of my life.

Berlin and Hitler's Death

The German high command spent April 20th celebrating Hitler's 56th birthday; he confidently told them that Russia would suffer its greatest defeat at the gates of Berlin. At this point, the Russians and Western Allies were in a position to block any escape to the south.

The majority of Hitler's administrative staff had abandoned Berlin in a frantic exodus moving south. They presumed that Hitler would follow the others immediately, but he procrastinated and stayed in Berlin. He knew the difficulty of holding Berlin with the Russians closing in. Yet he was self-delusional that his armies could yet achieve a spectacular victory and save their capital.

Hitler would yell and complain that the German people failed him and deserved whatever cruel treatment they got from the conquering Russians. This in fact would be payback for the torturous brutality of German troops on Russian civilians.

He would then rail against his incompetent, spineless, and negligent generals who were fools and fatheads. He was intolerant when a general spoke the truth, giving him information he did not want to hear.

By 23 April, the Russians had surrounded Berlin and were pounding it with artillery.

Reichsmarshal Goering learned that Hitler had stayed in Berlin. Having been designated Hitler's successor, he believed it was time to attempt to negotiate peace terms with the Allies. He radioed a message to Hitler from Berchtesgaden in Bavaria for instructions. By that evening he had received no reply and assumed the worst had happened and that Hitler had been taken by the Russians. He thus attempted to take control of Germany.

Hitler was thrown into a rage when he received Goering's message. Hitler demanded Goering's resignation from the command of the Luftwaffe and the Nazi party for "high treason." The next day, he was arrested by the SS.

On April 25, Russian and American troops met at a crossing on the Elbe River, west of the German capital. The Western and Eastern Fronts had joined.

Hitler's decision to stay in Berlin until the end created an air of silent resignation only relieved by an occasional vein of hope. By now his entourage was aware that Hitler intended to commit suicide along with Eva Braun.

The Russian artillery falling in the Reich Chancellery Garden above the bunker told them the end was near. The Führer's military chiefs, Alfred Jodl and Wilhelm Keitel, were not in the bunker but continued to report the military situation to Hitler. They either colored the reports or refused to face the facts themselves.

News poured into the bunker on April 28th, none of it good. Italian partisans had arrested Benito Mussolini, and there were rumors that army leaders were negotiating surrender in Italy. Both Mussolini and his mistress were executed and hung upside down by their heels.

The next day was worse. General Wenck's Twelfth Army stalled near Potsdam, 17 miles south of Berlin. Wenck was counting on the 30,000 men of the Ninth Army who had escaped the Russian encirclement of Berlin to help save the Reich. However, they were exhausted, low on weapons and ammunition, and of no help to his Twelfth Army. There would be no rescue.

Unbeknownst to Hitler, Heinrich Himmler had been negotiating with Swedish Count Bernadotte of the Red Cross. Himmler had written to Eisenhower that Germany was willing to surrender to the Western Powers but would continue to fight the Russians until the Allies assumed the fight against Bolshevism.

Hitler was devastated to discover, through a monitored broadcast of the BBC, that Himmler, too, had turned traitor. Himmler, like Goering, was expelled from the party and stripped of any claim to succession.

Hitler drew up a will and named Admiral Karl Doenitz as the new head of Germany and Supreme Commander of all armed forces.

Early on April 30th, Hitler married Eva Braun. By then he had concluded it was time to take his own life. He spent the morning saying farewell to the staff. When he and Eva retired to his suite, Russian troops were little more than a block away.

Eva Braun killed herself by biting on a cyanide capsule. Hitler shot himself with a pistol. In accordance with prior instructions, members of the household staff burned the bodies outside the bunker. Per Lev Aleksandrovich Bezymensky, *The Death of Adolf Hitler* (New York: Harcourt, Brace & World, 1968)

Move to the Elbe River

On May 2nd, the three Combat Commands of the 7th Armored traveled 100 miles from Eschede to Vellahn, crossing the Elbe River. The next day, Jack and his company were on patrol and unexpectedly encountered Russian forces. Such encounters had been common along the Elbe since the initial meeting between American and Russian forces on April 25th.

> Our encounter was with a tank unit, their Sherman tanks bearing battle scars, commanded by a woman. At first, their Tommy guns were aimed at us, a stark display of hostility. Yet, the moment they recognized us as American tankers, the atmosphere changed dramatically. Hostility melted away, replaced by cheers and embraces, and we started to believe this damn war was close to ending.

Once again assigned to the Second British Army, Jack's Company C worked with the 7th Battalion of the Scottish Black Watch (Royal

Highland Regiment), historically one of the most renowned British combat battalions.

The Germans had called them the "Ladies from Hell" in World War I; their fearless fighting in kilts was a testament to their bravery.

Jack wrote, "They were a pleasure to fight with. At 3 p.m. in the afternoon, regardless of what was happening, they stopped for tea. It was a most pleasant experience."

They had just captured the German airfield at Tarnewitz together. Originally, it was a Luftwaffe weapons testing facility built on an artificial peninsula on the Baltic Sea. After it was captured by Company C and the Ladies of the Black Watch, it was turned over to B Company of the 33rd Armored Engineering Battalion. They tirelessly worked to establish a POW camp for the Germans so they could consolidate all the prisoners remaining in the area.

Jack's Company and the Black Watch moved west across the peninsula to Dassow, where Task Force Dailey had established its headquarters. The center of the highways were full of German POWs marching toward the town.

After Major Dailey set up a POW enclosure, by the following morning, over 4,000 prisoners were under guard. Jack described it:

> In early May of 1945, with little warning, we were deluged by thousands of German troops surrendering to us and fleeing the Russians. The movement was so great that tanks were stationed at corners of fields, prisoners guided through to stack weapons, and then on to POW fields. The problem was how to feed 20,000 prisoners. Solution: we commandeered all bakeries in the region to bake bread. Water, hygiene, and food problems were managed.
>
> The Burgermeisters in the various towns were forced to furnish food and billets for all displaced personnel and German refugees. Food for prisoners in the camps was obtained through the 7th Armored Division General Administration.

Major Dailey placed German officers and NCOs in charge of managing the troops. The Germans were forced to maintain a high standard of sanitation. German surgeons and sanitary corps enlisted men were organized and used to the maximum. In order to control lice and other insects, the Americans were compelled to sprinkle themselves with DDT powder. What was left over was gathered up and given to the German POWs to use.

The personnel in the POW enclosure were organized into companies and battalions. All available German field stoves were obtained, and companies cooked and issued the food.

The German military hospital at Dassow was taken over and put under American medical officer supervision. However, the German personnel remained in the hospital to do the work.

After several hectic days, Jack finally had a chance to write Jean and Peter on May 4th:

> It has been several days since I've been able to write you each evening when my thoughts are closest to you and home. Yet, you're always

Jack's Story | **185**

near to my heart and the deep love I have learned from you has been such a comfort and aid to me in those past days when one truly wonders if the war will ever end and if it were possible for a man to survive that battle. I believe the end is now in sight; at least all indications are in that direction, and when one can at last almost see their way clear, it brings to mind the many blessings we have had and are so appreciative of.

The British awarded Colonel Wemple the Distinguished Service Order the other day. It is next to the highest award made by the British, the highest being the Victoria Cross. He was awarded it for his action in the Bulge last December. Also, our chaplain, Captain Utter, was awarded the Croix de Guerre of the Second Order, the first being the highest, for his action as a chaplain under fire during the march through France.

I am sitting in a little town with the Company and a few tank destroyers. I am the Town Commandant, and in many ways, it is a very humorous job, although at times quite pathetic. German people were scared of the Russians. The first question they ask is, "Are the Rooskies coming here?" When we tell them they are, they start trembling and want to take off to the next town. They are afraid that the Russians are going to give them a little of the same treatment that they so kindly donated to the Russians themselves for the past several years.

One man in this town beat up two Polish girls several times in the period that they have been forced to work for him, so when I heard about it, I sent a man down there and told him that if he ever so much as laid a hand on them again, I would cut off both his hands and then kill him. We haven't seen him anymore. It sounds rough, yet it is the only language that these perverts understand.

You would be amazed at the manner in which the people are fleeing from their homes and towns. They seem to have lost all sense of reason and are so full of polluted German propaganda that they all believe they are going to be killed. Sometimes, I don't think that would be too bad for them. I truly hope that I never again see people as starved, mistreated, and thoroughly abused as some of those allied prisoners, slave laborers, and, above all, those confined in the concentration camps were treated. It really makes you see red! Yes, that is enough shop talk from Johnny, eh?

Over the next several days, More German soldiers drifted into the POW enclosure at Dassow and the camp established at the Tarnewitz airfield. Various units of the 7th Armored Division, including Jack's Company C, were systematically going door to door in the different villages and towns to search for troops and remove any armaments and ammunition, which was then taken to a site for destruction. All enemy vehicles were also driven or towed to a maintenance lot for destruction.

Germany Surrenders

On May 5th, a German contingent from Admiral Doenitz met in Reims, France, with General Eisenhower's SHAEF group and Maj. Gen. Ivan Susloparoff, the Soviet liaison officer to SHAEF, to represent Soviet interests in any negotiations with the Doenitz government. General Alfred Jodl represented Germany.

The Germans were told that the surrender would occur simultaneously on the Eastern and Western fronts. This was telegraphed by Jodl back to Doenitz, requesting permission either to sign an unconditional surrender for all fronts or to have someone else come to Reims for that purpose.

The Germans, primarily Jodl, were attempting to stall surrender on the Eastern front, to allow more Germans to escape safely beyond Western lines and away from the Russians.

On the night of May 6th, the SHAEF negotiator went directly to the Supreme Commander about the German delaying tactics. "If the Germans did not speedily agree to the terms," Eisenhower responded, "he would break off all negotiations and seal the Western Front, preventing by force any further westward movement of German soldiers and civilians."

Impressed with Eisenhower's determination, Jodl cabled Doenitz for authority to accept the terms of surrender on all fronts.

On May 7th, in the War Room of Eisenhower's Headquarters in a red brick boys' school, the terms of surrender were signed by General Jodl. For the benefit of the Russians, on May 8th, General Keitel signed a copy of the same document in Berlin. The surrender would come into effect on May 8th, 1945, at 11:01 p.m.

CHAPTER TWENTY-ONE

Can't Wait to Go Home

While everyone at home was told that Germany had surrendered, VE-Day in Europe was almost anti-climactic to the troops. There were no huge celebrations, as everyday duties continued to keep everyone busy. Jack's Company C was moved to Selmsdorf, 12 miles west of Dassow, where they established a Military Government office.

The company searched the area for German soldiers, vehicles, weapons, ammunition, and other equipment. A large amount was collected and taken to Dassow for disposal. Selmsdorf had 60 police officers who were assigned to block the eastern boundary to stop any refugees or movement of displaced people into the area.

Jack's company had relieved a British major of his command. The Brits had shot several individuals the night before who were threatening the security of the town, so it was a little wild. After the GIs got into position it quieted down; hopes were that it would stay that way.

There was a nice beach nearby, and with the help of German POWs it was cleaned up for the Allied troops to swim. Jack laughed about the last several days being so hot because, during the Bulge, he swore he would never again complain about hot weather since it was so cold then. The only issue was that the lack of adequate bathing facilities made it difficult to keep "sweet and clean" in warm weather, so swimming was a convenient way to bathe. The days were long, with darkness coming

Jack's Story | **189**

after 10:00 p.m. "We have very short nights here, which is nice because they can work us longer daily!"

There were several trips into Lubeck, ten miles west of Selmsdorf. Jack thought the city was the most beautiful he had yet seen and had very little damage. In a letter he told Jean, "The women are really on the beam to look at. 'Army Wives, Inc.' must have instituted this non-fraternization program. One can't be blamed for looking, though, or can they?"

Jack had just found out that he had been recommended for promotion to Captain. The promotion had gone to the division but bounced because of an excess of Captains. Oh well, he sighed, "c'est la guerre-sky!"

The surrender agreement signed on May 8th established various occupation zones. Everything east of the Elbe River was Russian. Various Western Allied troops had to relocate into their own occupation zones. Part of the agreement actually froze anyone in a Russian zone from moving to a Western zone. This would become Eastern Europe. Winston Churchill later coined a phrase for the new situation when he said, "From Stettin in the Baltic, to Trieste in the Adriatic, an *iron curtain* has descended across the continent." The establishment of this border ushered in the Cold War and framed the geo-political landscape for the next 50 years.

Relocated to the American Zone

On May 20th, the 17th Tank Battalion was moved from the Dassow area, a Russian zone, 260 miles west to Glesien, Germany. The area was largely farmland and the food supply was good. The battalion spent the next few days getting all its units in place and billeted.

Jack wrote to Jean that Glesien was in between Halle and Leipzig, on the west side of the Saale River. The Russians would control the east side, including Leipzig, when it became East Germany in 1949. He was looking forward to getting down to visit that famous city. "Most of these

German cities have had their hearts bombed out of them," he wrote, "literally and figuratively."

Joseph Goebbels, Hitler's Information Minister, had continually broadcast propaganda to the German people about how evil the Russian army was, scaring the population to its bones. They were told that the Russians would rape the women, kill civilians, and pillage the countryside wherever they went. Many of the Russians were indeed brutal and horrendous. The truth, which the German citizens had no knowledge of, was that the German Army had done precisely the same when they invaded Russia.

Before the war ended, knowing the Russians were coming, much of the civilian population had been terrified as the Russians moved west. Germans crowded the roads with their few possessions. They had deserted their homes, leaving anything they could not carry, and headed west to the safety of the American lines.

The Americans had little sympathy for the German citizens because of the horrific way the Nazis had treated those in the concentration and POW camps and the slave laborers from France, Holland, Belgium, Poland, Russia, and the Balkans. While many of these citizens had nothing to do with what had happened during the war, many stood by and let it happen.

Jack's friend Chris Chrisman, the division logistics officer, had to return and pick up some equipment left in Dassow. The Germans begged him to take them to the American area.

Jack wrote home:

> Halle left much to be desired, namely running water, paved streets, a few of the comforts we know at home, etc. In some ways, the German people are highly modern with their excellent autobahn highways, well-constructed housing projects, etc. Yet, when one gets ten miles off a main highway, he finds himself in communities living the same life as has been going on for the past ten centuries with dairy cattle pulling carts, women and children working the fields (no machinery),

huge manure piles in front of each house. Why do our men have to walk down the streets in pairs? So that if they fall into a manure pile, there will be someone there to pull them out. Stinks too. Lots of flies buzzing here and there.

Jack, as part of the Military Government, was assigned to handle a complaint from some local German civilians. They complained that Polish people were coming into the area from Leipzig and stealing hogs and cattle.

The investigation revealed that the Poles had paid the farmers a good price for the livestock. To avoid this type of manipulation by the Germans in the future, the Poles were told they must buy the livestock through the Military Government office. The office had to deal with these and other petty complaints, but there had been no serious trouble.

A few weeks after Victory in Europe Day, the company finally had the chance to celebrate. Jack wrote to Jean about their belated celebration:

> This evening, we're going to have a company party. We were issued several bottles of cognac, champagne, and wine for the men, serving as our VE day celebration.
>
> John Zanone, my executive officer, received a letter yesterday from stateside saying they didn't blame us for having a good time on VE day. We got a big kick out of that because we were bivouacked out in a dirty old field and still capturing Jerry. We were all slightly envious of our 4F brothers for bending ze elbows for us! C'est la guerre, I say once again.

Jack told Jean and his parents the story of their new flag:

> We now have an American flag in our company. We are not entitled to an issued flag, so we had one made. White from a sheet, red from a Nazi flag, and blue from a frau's skirt. Two German women sewed it for us and did a beautiful job. It was just finished this evening, we

will have a little ceremony when we raise it. Too bad we can't get an issued flag, but this is quite nice.

The labor costs here are extremely low. The hourly rate for labor is equivalent to 2-1/2 cents American money. Unions would have a field day here. A woman washed and pressed my laundry. I gave her five marks ($.50), which seemed like a fortune to her. We paid the "Betsy Ross" gals three dollars for sewing the flag. They worked on it for two days and now consider themselves rich.

Information and Education

After Lt. Colonel Wemple had selected Jack to run the Information and Education program for the 17th Tank Battalion in February, there was little they could do during combat, with the exception of some correspondence courses through the University of Wisconsin that some in the battalion signed up for.

With the war over, however, and the men on "occupation" duty, there was more time for those who wanted to take courses. Jack said, "This I and E job of mine is really developing into something. We have a staff of three men, including myself, here at headquarters, three men, and an officer in each company. It really keeps us hoping to keep up with everything."

Colonel Wemple had Jack move up to Battalion HQ to live. He became the staff's assistant S-3 (Operations and Training) officer while still commanding C Company. With the time at HQ, he didn't have the time to be around the company as much as he should have. There was much work in both areas and too little time in the day to accomplish it all.

As part of the I&E program, Jack ran trips to the Nazi concentration camp at Buchenwald. It was essential that as many men in the command as possible witness what the Polish, Russians, Jews, French, and others went through as inmates. They had to see the blood-stained walls, the huge crematories, the filthy "hospital," and the rest that went with it. Visiting Buchenwald gave the men a sense that they did not fight only to defeat the Germans but to save as many lives as possible from the horror and death of these camps. Jack often thought about his visit to Bergen-Belsen on May 1st and how it offended and sickened him.

With the war over, Jack also had the chance to see and do things that being in combat didn't allow, such as travel to various towns and cities.

Jack, Chris Chrisman, and Larry Deutsch, the battalion's Chief Warrant Officer (CFW), took Jack's jeep into Leipzig to see the city and take pictures. The city was spectacular and had little damage. They had a great time with lunch and some good beer.

On the way out of Leipzig, MPs pulled them over and arrested them for the offense of all three of them riding in the front of the jeep. Nothing would come of it, but Chris, having the highest date-of-rank, was given the ticket. Jack had commented several times about the difference between being out on the front lines and being back amid the spit and polish of non-combat commands. Welcome back to that world.

Jack acquired a three-day pass to Paris and traveled with the Battalion Maintenance officer, Ernie Stanley. They were looking forward to the glamorous high life of Paris while there, as life in Germany at its best was not too sharp.

Unfortunately, the weather was wet, but that didn't dampen the fun and joy. One evening they ran into a French friend of Jack's named Charles, whom he had met at the Information and Education school in March.

Charles insisted that his sister, Babette, take Ernie and Jack sightseeing and shopping the next day. They enjoyed the beautiful city and commented on how nicely the women were dressed. Jack wanted to buy something for Jean but couldn't find anything she might have liked.

Charles was quite wealthy and from a very upstanding family. Their home was two blocks from the Eiffel Tower, next to a beautiful park. On the last night in Paris, they were invited to their home for dinner, and it was really out of this world. A butler and maid served the seven courses. Ernie and Jack actually had to watch the others to see which fork or spoon to use.

After three days, they had consumed *beaucoup* champagne and were ready for a return to their troops in Germany.

On a Sunday afternoon, Larry Deutsch and Jack drove to Heidelberg. They wanted to see the University of Heidelberg, as it was quite famous; the operetta "The Student Prince" was written with the University of Heidelberg as the setting. Jack was quite disappointed when they saw it, as the school was in the middle of town, and the buildings were separated only by the city streets. The campuses of American universities far surpassed those seen over here.

The old castle, Heidelberg Schloss, was situated on a huge hill overlooking the city and the beautiful valley that opens into the Rhine River valley a few miles away. They visited the castle, walked around the grounds, took several pictures, and were about to go inside when a German civilian asked them for their tickets! That was too much for them. They turned around and walked off. "Can you imagine them charging Americans to see their stinky castle after we liberated them a couple of months ago? I can't see it myself."

Even with this break to travel to cities in Europe, Jack missed Jean and his son more and more every day, but duty was not over.

The Point System

The military used a point system established in September 1944 to determine eligibility for returning home. When Germany surrendered to the Allies on May 8, 1945, the US Army faced the enormous task of transitioning the largest field army in its history. This included forming an occupation force in Europe, redeploying soldiers for the expected invasion of Japan, and discharging millions of men who had fought in Europe.

Points were awarded according to the following formula, with 85 points needed to go home:

1. *Service Duration:* One point for each month of service in the Army.

2. *Overseas Service:* One additional point for each month in service overseas.

3. *Campaign Participation:* Five points for each campaign.

4. *Medals for Valor:* Five points for a medal for merit or valor (e.g., Silver Star).

5. *Wounds Received:* Five points for a Purple Heart (awarded for wounds).

6. *Dependents:* Twelve points for each dependent child, up to three children.

Jack had been thinking about his points and writing about them to Jean and his parents. He needed 85 points and currently had 56.

> I'm glad I didn't go into the service sooner than I did because God only knows where I'd be now, yet I would have many more points. At any rate, looking at the situation as it exists today, I have 56 points with a possibility of getting 10 more for the Battle of the Bulge and east of the Rhine. That will bring the total to 66, which isn't many, but still quite a few. Little Peter John came through with 12 points for the old man, not bad for such a youngster!

Choices and Opportunities

Jack reflected: "I'm 24 years old and apparently good military material for a while anyway. I expect it will not be weeks but months before I leave the ETO unless I should be sent to a 'hot' outfit for the CBI. (CBI is China, Burma, India Theater.)"

With so few points, Jack had three possible outcomes. He had made up his mind not to make the Army his career, so it was best to examine the choices available:

First: Occupation duty in the ETO.

Second: CBI ("I hope not!")

Third: Return home with some outfits and remain there as Strategic Reserve. He could be redeployed to the Pacific or CBI, but he would first enjoy a leave at home.

Colonel Wemple and Major Dailey had been helping him find steady positions and believed his family could join him. But Jack thought bringing Jean and Peter would be unfair to their son, with his medical issues.

Moves on to Graves Registration

A quota came in for some officers to be transferred to ETOUSA in the Quartermaster Corps. Jack never had too much respect for some men in that particular branch, as it always seemed to be an excellent way to keep from being shot at.

Only officers with combat experience were qualified to apply. Jack's CO, Colonel Wemple, and Exec, Major Dailey of the 17th Tank Battalion, thought it foolish to pass up such an opportunity. They said that Jack had been shot at enough.

He applied and was selected for Quartermaster School on July 18th. "It is nice to escape Germany for a while, but I miss the old outfit. The Colonel sent an excellent recommendation, so I must do my best now." His first assignment was to Graves Registration in Paris.

Before he left, the Executive Officer of Company C, John Zanone, presented Jack with the American flag made by the German team "Betty Ross." When he returned to the US, the flag was always hung on a wall in his home and honored by the whole family. When he spent his final year at the California Veterans Home in Napa Valley, he honored the home by donating the flag to his fellow veterans.

Graves Registration has been active as far back as the early 1800s. Quartermaster officers assigned to frontier outposts constructed cemetery plots and buried the dead in marked graves and kept a fairly uniform burial record. The effort to properly care for individuals who died in battle grew during the Civil War and the Spanish-American War. In 1912, the Quartermaster Department was reorganized and became the

Quartermaster Corps, where specialized troops took over most of the functions previously performed by civilians or detachments from the line.

General Pershing established a Graves Registration Service in 1918 to care for the dead in World War I. GRREG companies offered close support to the line, including establishing temporary cemeteries in local areas. The dedication and spirit of member personnel were often noteworthy to the point of extremes. No risk appeared too dangerous or effort too great if it promised identification of a "buddy's" remains. General Pershing wrote of one particular unit's activities in the spring of 1918:

> (They) began their work under heavy artillery fire and gas, and, although troops were in dugouts, these men immediately went to the cemetery and, in order to preserve records and locations, repaired and erected new crosses as fast as old ones were blown down. They also completed the extension to the cemetery. During that time, shells were falling continuously, and they were subjected to mustard gas. They gathered many bodies that had been first in the hands of the Germans and were later retaken by American counterattacks. Identification was especially difficult, all papers and tags having been removed, and most of the bodies being in a terrible condition and beyond recognition.

Families could choose for their fallen to be returned to the States for burial, but many relatives of soldiers opted to have their kin remain in the country where they had fallen. Teddy Roosevelt added impetus to this movement by requesting that his son, Lieutenant Quentin Roosevelt, be buried near the ground where he was killed. His expression – "Where the tree falls, let it lie" – echoed the sentiments of many. Eight permanent cemeteries were established, and 30,000 veterans were laid to rest.

The Quartermaster Graves Registration Service reduced the percentage of unknowns to less than three bodies for every hundred recovered.

While organizational and operational refinements helped reduce the time between original burial and final disposition of remains, a new and more scientific approach aided immeasurably in the identification process. World War I saw the coming of age of Army graves registration.

During World War II, the task of registering graves proved far greater. More than 250,000 Americans died and were buried in temporary cemeteries around the world. On the European continent alone, fighting had scattered dead US servicemen over a million and a half square miles of territory, making the recovery process more difficult. Lost airmen were especially widespread and difficult to locate. Further, new weapons (including aerial bombardment and massive use of artillery) often rendered those killed in action unrecognizable.

The standard Graves Registration Company in World War II consisted of 260 men and five officers. It was intended to support three divisions, one platoon per division. Each platoon was divided into two sections – a collecting squad and an evacuation squad. GRREG companies collected, evacuated, identified, and supervised the burial of the dead. These field units also collected and disposed of personal effects and, subject to the approval of higher headquarters, selected sites for temporary cemeteries. As in World War I, work was often done under extremely hazardous conditions.

Another example of heroic service can be found in the record of a Quartermaster Graves Registration Company that scrambled ashore on D-Day with the First Army. There they gathered bodies from the beaches, in the water, and inland, actually cutting many from wrecked landing craft submerged in the shallow water. By the end of D-plus 2, one platoon alone had buried 457 Americans; by working day and night, the three platoons had been able to clear the beaches of all remains.

Total Disarray

Jack's initial reaction to the Graves Registration organization in Paris was that it consisted of people who didn't care and acted very dispiritedly.

"Everything is disorganized, and some officers rule with an iron fist while others do as little as they can. I can't say that I enjoy the thought of fighting the war and then cleaning it up afterward. I'm a field soldier at heart! I enjoy being with the men."

Jack was unaware of what was happening behind the scenes with the whole structure of Graves Registration. However, he knew he had a job to accomplish and would do his best to accomplish the mission when assigned the responsibility.

General Robert Littlejohn was the Chief Quartermaster for the European Theater of Operations (ETO). With the war over, he was concerned that the Paris office of Graves Registration was not following his directions to regionalize operations away from Paris. He had an Inspector General's report done on the Paris office, and it was devastating. Littlejohn summarized: "My Graves Registration and Effects Division is entrenched behind the ramparts of Paris, sitting on its fanny smoking big cigars and dreaming about something that may or may not happen.... Last week, we had the Inspector General in on this project. I found the Effects Depot is still in Paris after I ordered it to move weeks ago."

General Littlejohn went to Eisenhower and Bradley to request the appointment of General James W. Younger, the former QM, 12th Army Group, as chief of the Graves Registration and Effects Division, effective August 2nd, while remaining a member of Littlejohn's staff.

Reorganization

Younger concentrated on setting up a five-zone territorial organization, mainly to care for the cemeteries on the Continent and in the United Kingdom. He first assumed command of the field unit at Fulda, Germany, to conduct a sweep of Germany, Poland, and Czechoslovakia. He continued to strengthen the other four zones while he built his team.

Jack was with another officer at the motor pool trying to get a vehicle when he ran into General Younger, his commanding general. He started to talk with us and said:

"Wilson, how many points do you have?" I answered, "74, Sir," and he said, "How much of a family have you?" And I told him of my wonderful wife and child. I wondered what he was driving at but didn't have long to wait. He asked me if I would stay here and help get the ball rolling for him. He said he thought your wife would like it over here and would be able to come this spring. I replied that I appreciated his offer very much and would happily help them until my ship was ready to sail. He asked me to consider it, and I said, "Yes, sir."

General Younger wasted no time putting Jack on his team to "get the ball rolling," understanding Jack would depart when he could finally go home.

Over the next six months, Jack got involved in working around the problems caused by Washington DC, trying to combine the management of all Grave Registration in the three theaters: Europe, Mediterranean/Middle East, and Pacific together. General Younger was given the Mediterranean/Mideast on top of Europe and, with Littlejohn's concurrence, ignored it to concentrate on his five zones.

Because of the point system and transfers to other theaters, there was a significant shortage of men. Even more serious was that few officers and men remaining with the units were experienced and technically qualified. There were a few trainers available in the theater. Jack's first job was to fix the training program while others worked on getting it staffed. Graves Registration Command was assured by Washington that 7,244 officers and men, about evenly divided between green recruits and transfers from the antiaircraft artillery, would be available until 1 July 1946; that number was reduced substantially to 2,500, but they drifted in slowly.

General Younger had his team concentrate on getting the five European zones operational and efficient. On V-E Day, approximately 117,000 Americans were buried in fifty-four temporary cemeteries. Over the next eleven months, the number of cemeteries had been reduced to thirty-six, and it was estimated that with other recovery efforts, the total number of burials would be over 148,000.

The other challenge was dealing with the next of kin regarding whether the family member would be laid to rest in one of the European or British cemeteries or repatriated back home. The final result was that some 41 percent of the 146,000 ultimately recovered, or approximately 60,000, remained in the ETO, and were eventually buried at the ten sites proposed by Graves Registration Command.

Jack enjoyed working with General Younger and was promoted to Captain in October. He later told Jean that the challenges and pace of work made those final months seem a little shorter.

Jack gained tremendous respect for the efforts of the frontline technicians and workers in identifying individuals in the temporary graves and for the respect and honor they received in their treatment. He often thought about those comrades he lost during the Battle of the Bulge and the Ruhr Pocket, such as Louie Brodman, S/Sgt. Bill Crutcher, and others.

Who would have imagined that a young man just completing his college adventure would spend the next two years of his life fighting in the most devastating war of the modern era? He was only 24 years old; he had faced death, seen his friends killed, and made difficult decisions that affected all the men in his unit and the outcomes in many battles. He still had his entire life ahead of him; like many of the men who made it through this war, Jack never talked about what had happened until his later years.

Jack reached the "Magic 85" points in January of 1946 and was able to start the trip back home. He shipped out of Le Havre, France on the 30th of January for New York, arriving on the 11th of February. With all the returning troops, the rail system had to be used, and he departed New York for Chicago with a changeover to Fort Douglas in Salt Lake City. He was then sent by train to Portland, Oregon. He took a local the final 130 miles to Fort Lewis, Washington, for final discharge from the Army on the 24th of February.

He finally arrived home to hold his son Peter and his loving wife the next day in Spokane.

Jean's parents, Han and Nell, held a welcome-home party for Jack with his parents, "Poppa John" and Esther. The party was also a late celebration of Peter's first birthday. The day was very festive, with a drink or two.

Jack had developed a love for cognac, especially in Paris, and he had carried a special old bottle of Hennessy for Jean and him to enjoy when they bought a home in Seattle and settled in. Han and Poppa John learned about the bottle and wanted to taste it.

The two of them giggled the evening away as they polished off the whole bottle!

Jack loved to tell that story.

Jack's Ending Note

John C. Wilson., Jr.
1371 Bonita Bahia Benicia, CA 94150

July 5, 1995
TO WHOM IT MAY CONCERN:

In May, my dear friend Frank Taylor wrote to me, "My real family... and my near family should have some kind of a transcript of my experiences, trials, and tribulations that I experienced in the armored conflict in World War II."

A year ago, I received the enclosed letter from my son John, who is also a veteran.

My report is a chronicle of some of the major actions. Others include a firefight with a German panzer where my superior Platoon Sergeant was blown to bits in his tank next to me. God Bless Staff Sgt. Bill Crutcher! Others include my gunner, Louie Brodman, shot by a sniper as we were loading shells for our cannon. Then, too, was the confrontation I had with a German SS officer in a captured village. I ordered him to surrender, he pulled his sidearm, and I killed him. One of the worst experiences was in a captured village at dusk after a firefight. Houses were burning, and I was told women and children were in the cellar of a burning house. There was no way to get them out, so I ordered a tank to fire a high explosive shell into the cellar; it was not a very nice experience.

As I watch the current generation of youngsters grow up with little or no expression of patriotism, I am developing a deep concern about to whom we are entrusting the future of our great nation. I believe that God will provide. I shall not have to worry about it.

John C. Wilson, Jr.

September 11, 2001

Again, a despicable surprise attack was launched against America. Like Jack's generation after Pearl Harbor, American men and women from all walks of life volunteered to go to war to defend our country from an enemy that wanted America brought to its knees.

Jack died in 1997 and would have been one month short of his 80th birthday on 9/11. Nevertheless, he would have stood at attention and saluted the modern generation with tears of pride in his eyes, recognizing the same surge of patriotism his own generation had shown. God Bless all of you!